lola donation    $ 24 ⁹⁵

# FAILURE IS NOT AN OPTION

To
Ruth Ann,
Wishing You
great Success!

Donna Jordan

Thanks

# FAILURE IS
# NOT
## AN OPTION

## 10 SURE-FIRE STEPS TO
## SUCCESS

BY

DONNA JORDAN

CRANBERRY COVE PUBLISHERS  SPRINGBORO OHIO

Cranberry Cove Publishers
P.O. Box 606
Springboro, Ohio 45066

Printed in the United States of America
First edition January 1998
10 9 8 7 6 5 4 3 2 1

Editor: Chris Roerden
Cover Design: George Foster
Cover Photo: AGI Photographic Imaging, Miamisburg, OH
Photo Stylist: Pamela VanderVort
Interior Illustrations: Dan Harman

Library of Congress Card Catalog Number 97-69667

Publisher's Cataloging-in-Publication

Jordan, Donna, 1949-
    Failure is not an option : 10 sure-fire steps to succcess / by
Donna Jordan. -- 1st ed.
        p. cm.
        Includes bibliographical references and index.
        ISBN: 0-9658020-2-7 HC

    1. Success.  2. Broadcast journalism--Biography.  3. Jordan,
Donna, 1949-  I. Title.

BF637.S8J67 1998                         158
                                    QBI97-41088

*Charles Osgood and Donna Jordan*

## TO THE READER

Donna Jordan's career as a television journalist and news anchor has been successful by anybody's measure. Her work has earned her national honors and the respect of her professional colleagues all across the country.

Donna has a way of getting to the heart of a story, making what is interesting, important, and what is important, fascinating. In the process, Donna Jordan has learned a great deal, not only about television and reporting but also about herself.

In this remarkable book she shows us specific step-by-step methods to turn fear into confidence and confidence into success, no matter what we do. Although her examples come from the same crazy TV jungle that I inhabit, Donna's lessons are so down-to-earth and universal they can be applied by anyone in any walk of life to achieve whatever goals we may set for ourselves. If you are just starting out, it's not too early—and if you are well along the road, as I am, it is not too late—to enjoy and profit from Donna Jordan's encouraging and well-chosen words.

At heart, *FAILURE IS NOT AN OPTION* isn't about succeeding in television or journalism. It's about succeeding in life.

—*Charles Osgood*
*Anchor, CBS News' SUNDAY MORNING*

## TO THE READER

In addition to your being entertained by the exciting story of a journalist's varied life—including encounters with celebrities—you will be inspired by *FAILURE IS NOT AN OPTION.*

Here you will learn special strategies that will fuel your own journey to success.

Donna Jordan's success has not come without courageous risks, honest mistakes, and tough lessons learned. In this entertaining and educational book, she spotlights the specific obstacles she overcame and the skills she acquired to do so.

Donna Jordan's book is a gift, and a delightful and provocative read.

—*Susan Page, Author*
***HOW ONE OF YOU CAN BRING***
***THE TWO OF YOU TOGETHER***
*and*
***IF I'M SO WONDERFUL, WHY AM I STILL SINGLE?***

# CONTENTS

ACKNOWLEDGMENTS ............................................. ix

**CHAPTER**

**1** It Begins with Leadership ............................................. 1

**2** . . . And Ends with Success ........................................ 15

**3** STEP ONE: Plunge in with a Positive
& Courageous Attitude ............................................. 33

**4** STEP TWO: Step Out with a Strong Self-Image ...... 55

**5** STEP THREE: Lengthen Your Stride with Self-
Motivation & Willingness to Change .................... 77

**6** STEP FOUR: Clear All Obstacles from Your Path .. 95

**7** STEP FIVE: Pick Up the Pace with Confidence .... 125

**8** STEP SIX: Communicate Carefully ........................ 143

**9** STEP SEVEN: Focus Your Vision ........................... 175

**10** STEP EIGHT: Goals Will Get You There ................ 197

**11** STEP NINE: Build Your Reputation on Character 223

**12** STEP TEN: Dig In with Determination .................. 241

A FINAL NOTE ............................................................ 265

INDEX ........................................................................ 275

RESOURCES ............................................................... 278

# WORKSHEETS

**1** List Your Talents, Strengths, Abilities ...................... 22

**2** Adjectives to Describe Me ............................................. 64

**3** What Motivates You? ..................................................... 82

**4** What's Holding You Back? ............................................ 98

**5** Start Talking Smart ......................................................117

**6** "Doughnut Game" ........................................................ 154

**7** Finding Your Vision ..................................................... 184

**8** My Vision ...................................................................... 195

**9** Goals Will Get Me There .............................................. 216

**10** My Personal Code of Ethics ........................................ 231

# ILLUSTRATIONS

How Many Balls Can You Juggle? ................................... 187

You Stop Dropping the Ball .............................................. 193

# ACKNOWLEDGMENTS

Thank you seems such a tiny phrase in reward for the wonderful support I've received in writing this book. I would like to thank Stephen Mitchell who assisted me with the content of this book. An expert in leadership and empowerment issues, Stephen helped me through some of the leadership areas I had yet to work out. Before I met Stephen, I would sometimes stew about every wrong, slight, or offensive action taken against me. It was he who offered solutions and encouraged me to write down in book form the most instructive of these experiences to help keep other women from falling into some of the same traps I had. I always knew I had a book in me, but it was Stephen who encouraged me to become committed to completing it.

My deepest appreciation also goes to my editor, Chris Roerden of Edit It in Brookfield, Wisconsin. What a joy to find a professional who wanted only to enhance my product rather than change it. I feel she made a good book better. She cleaned up my copy without ever altering my message. For that I am grateful.

I want to thank Mom and Dad, Marilyn and Normand Desjardins, for allowing me to expose some of the details of our private lives in an effort to help other women. I know Mom cringed a bit from time to time as I exposed some of the less than stellar moments in our lives. But the sad moments are far outweighed by the joyous times we've experienced as a family. You did a great job raising me. I respect, admire, and love you both.

I also wish to thank Geena Davis's parents, Virginia and

Bill Davis, of Wareham, Massachusetts, for their strong support of me and my book; as well as Charles Osgood, Meredith Vieira, Faith Daniels, Joan Lukey, and Ellen Berry.

I would not have been able to publish this book without the kind permission of Andy Fisher, David Lipoff, and John Woodin—my bosses at Cox Broadcasting. Instead of viewing my project as something that could interfere with my work for them, they embraced it wholeheartedly, understanding how important it is for me to help other women find success.

Finally, I would like to thank the two strongest women in my life for helping me become the woman I am today—Barbara Noon-Borges and Joyce McGuane. On the bad days, they never allowed me to wallow in misery or feel sorry for myself. They forced me to move ahead when I often felt like quitting. On the good days, they shared my joy and celebrated with me. They stand beside me today as they did decades ago. I thank you both from the bottom of my heart.

—Donna Jordan

# CHAPTER 1

# IT BEGINS WITH LEADERSHIP

*"We are not interested in the possibilities of defeat."*

—*Queen Victoria*

One look at the fat, black clouds scudding across the sky made me wish I had never left the security of my bed. Those evil-looking clouds, ripe with snow, proved a nasty portent of things to come that sloppy, gray Chicago day when *PM Magazine* sent me on one of the toughest interviews of my life. As my plane from Milwaukee, Wisconsin, bounced through the turbulence to finally set down in a rocky landing at O'Hare, I looked over my notes one last time.

I was about to interview one of the most reluctant stars in Hollywood. The landmark movie *Kramer Vs. Kramer*, starring Dustin Hoffman and Meryl Streep, was about to open in theaters across the United States. It was already being touted as a potential Oscar winner, and its producers were

pushing Hoffman to do what he allegedly hated most—
meet the media to promote his new flick.

Hoffman's reputation of being difficult to interview had
reached my ears. My first flush of pride at being one of a
handful of journalists selected to question him quickly
turned to fear as I heard how he breakfasted on reporters,
unhesitatingly chewing them up and spitting them out.

However, I had done my homework. I was prepared—
except that what I'd found out made me feel worse. It was
an obscure note in a gossip rag claiming that Hoffman and
his wife were splitting up. Great, I thought; if he hates talking about the movie, how will I ever get him to reveal something so personal? But that's my job. I couldn't go home
without the information.

About ten reporters were scheduled to talk to Hoffman
that morning. Gene Siskel, of Siskel and Ebert fame, won
the coveted top spot in the lottery. I came in second. That
was good news. I had heard that Hoffman tires quickly,
becoming more visibly bored as the day wears on. And wear
on it does. Imagine talking to one reporter after another,
answering the same inane questions repeatedly. It's enough
to make a grown man scream, or at least belch in your face—
a behavior rumored to be one of Hoffman's tricks to throw
reporters off.

I made up my mind that would not happen to me. I swallowed my fear along with a dry bagel and stepped into the
lion's den. There he was, pacing the elegantly appointed
hotel room, dressed in a suit and tie from the waist up,
cutoffs and torn sneakers adorning his nether limbs. He
looked bigger than life, even though I, at 5'4", didn't have
to tilt my head much to meet his eyes, powerful orbs that
reflected boredom and an evil glint as he focused on his
next victim. I knew the first words out of my mouth would

set the tone for the interview. Hoffman scowled at me, obviously waiting to hear what foolish thing I would say. I decided upon the truth.

"Look," I said seriously, "you don't want to do this any more than I do. You're being forced into it and so am I. So as long as we're in this together, let's sit down and do the best we can." Then I smiled. "I promise, I'll try not to ask you any stupid questions."

The stillness grew deafening, and then the most wonderful boyish grin broke out on his face. "All right, way to go. Let's get to it!"

Get to it we did. Not only did we talk about the movie and—very candidly—about his impending divorce, but he also took time after the interview to generously tape a local promotion spot with me, telling everyone to "Watch Donna Jordan on *PM Magazine*. Hello Milwaukee, Donna sent me!"

My interview with Hoffman headlined *PM Magazine* shows across the nation that month. The national office selected my work over several other interviews with the star conducted by *PM* co-hosts in television markets larger than Milwaukee's. Just before my story hit the airwaves, the office called and told me Hoffman had appeared bored and unresponsive in every other interview but mine.

"What's your secret?" they asked. "How did you get him to talk openly when no one else could?"

The answer seems easy enough now. I gained Hoffman's respect by taking the lead and setting the ground rules. This proved a much different approach from most of that day's interviewers, who could barely see this "little big man" for all the stars in their eyes. While they fawned and simpered in the presence of this mega-star, I took charge of my emotions, took control of my environment, and took ownership of one of the best interviews of my life.

## TAKE CONTROL AND GO

The interview with Hoffman could have gone either way that stormy Chicago day, but I arrived back at the TV station in Milwaukee that evening a hero with the story in hand. I credit the years of experience already under my belt for my success with Hoffman. When I first started in the business I would never have had the courage to take the lead and tell a Hollywood star what to do. As a novice reporter, I probably would have allowed myself to be influenced by his public relations people, who had many years of experience under their belts, and who would tell you only what they wanted you to know about their client.

Through the years my career has thrown me into more difficult situations than many people face in a lifetime. It was very often sink or swim, as I got tossed into a tough assignment head first. In the twenty years I've been struggling to find success, I've been shoved around, squeezed out, beaten up emotionally, and pushed beyond my physical limits. Every experience has been a lesson.

No matter what the storybooks say, success doesn't come overnight. For me, finding success was a process that encompassed ten valuable steps. The result of that process is called "personal leadership."

## LEAD YOUR WAY TO SUCCESS

*Personal leadership is doing what you know is right and productive for you regardless of the obstacles you face or the opinions of others.* It's letting people know what you stand for, and—more important—what you won't stand for. It means standing firm on your beliefs and principles even if you stand alone. Leaders don't follow the whims and desires of others. They carve out their own paths instead and are not easily influenced by others.

The year was 1974, the place, New Bedford, Massachusetts, which lies within the Providence, Rhode Island, TV market, and I had just landed my first job in television. You'll notice I said "in" television, not "on" television. Lacking both the education and the obligatory years of experience, I spent my days hunched over typewriter keys in a basement, pounding out letters for the sales department instead of breaking exciting stories upstairs in the newsroom. My dream was to become a TV anchor, but the job I'd landed was secretary.

Still, I had a plan. By working at the television station, I had slipped my foot in the door. Next, all I had to do was kick it open. I was confident that the job would be my stepping stone to success. But possessing a vision only I could see, I suffered the slings and arrows of those who didn't share my dream.

People told me I was crazy. Moving from the secretarial pool to TV anchor was not done. Apparently there was a caste system, and I didn't belong to the right sect. You see, to be an anchor, you first need to be an anchor in a smaller TV market, or perhaps a reporter ready to move up—certainly not somebody's secretary.

Not having any knowledge of this, I naïvely believed I had a chance. I refused to listen to the chorus of no's and launched a campaign to pry open the broadcast door even more.

I kept my eyes open and my ears alert for any opportunity. One amazing day, word filtered downstairs that the news director was searching the country for the perfect female anchor. "Why not give it a shot?" I thought. "What have you got to lose?" Trying to become a star, I began by reaching for the moon.

Hardly anybody, it seemed, wished me well. Still, I kept

moving forward as the naysayers worked to hold me back. I refused to allow ridicule and cutting comments to sway me from my course. Even the news director got a hearty laugh at my application for the job. Nevertheless, he allowed me to try.

I don't remember much about sitting at the anchor desk that fateful day and reading the newscopy on the Teleprompter for the first time. But I do remember exactly how I felt as I watched the engineers play the audition tape back for me to view. I was stunned. I looked every inch an anchor. Even though I was green something was there—a certain spark called charisma. The news director saw it, too. He stopped laughing and told me how wonderful I looked.

I didn't get the job that day. But the defeat only heightened my desire to do what it took to become successful. It took all my courage to walk back downstairs with my head held high amid the jeers of my coworkers.

Friendless and lonely, I sat at my typewriter every day until another opportunity came along. One day I happened to spot the news director heading for the personnel office with a man he'd just hired. I recognized the newcomer as a reporter from the radio station located just down the street. It took me no more than fifteen minutes to formulate a plan and put it into action.

Quickly, I typed out a résumé on the office typewriter and left the building, ostensibly for lunch. However, instead of snacking, I summoned up all the courage I could and made tracks to the radio station down the street, where I was sure the reporter would be returning that afternoon to give notice.

I stormed in like a Nor'easter blowing up the New England coast and demanded to see the news director. Fear does that to you. His secretary had been told not to allow visitors, but after viewing my unshielded desire and desperation, she let me pass. I thanked her mightily and made my approach to the man in charge. I looked the news director in the eye and boldly told him it was about time he had a woman reporter/anchor on the air, and I was the woman he needed for the job. He informed me that I didn't have experience and he didn't have an opening. That's when I announced, "You will have a job very soon, and when you do I want the opportunity to try!"

Doing a poor job of suppressing his laughter, he politely told me to get lost. I left my name, telephone number, and one final request: "Don't forget, if something happens today, call me. Just give me a chance. I can do the job."

Exhilarated by my surge of self-confidence, I returned to my secretarial job. Never taking my eyes off the telephone, I willed it to ring. An hour later the call came.

"Well, you've already proved you can dig for a story. You found out about the job opening before I did. You've earned your right to try. C'mon back."

During my afternoon coffee break I scooted back to the radio station. The news director handed me several sheets of Associated Press wire copy and asked me to read into a microphone while he taped my audition.

Wire copy was a frightening thing in those days. It had little or no punctuation, and I was reading it cold. I did great until the point where I announced, "Members of the aflcio today . . . ." Realizing "aflcio" was not a word, I quickly corrected myself. "Ah . . . that's the AFL-CIO . . ." and went on from there.

I passed the audition, even with the faux pas. However, I was clueless about the next part of my test—how to write newscopy. Thinking fast about how to buy myself more time, I explained I still owed allegiance to my present job and must return without delay. Innocently I asked, "May I take the copy with me, write the stories at my desk this afternoon, and drop them off to you after work?" The news director said "Yes," apparently forgetting where I worked.

As soon as I returned to the television station, I flew up the stairs, barged into the news director's office, and begged for his help. He remembered the potential shown by my anchor audition and understood this was my big break. He kindly showed me precisely what to do, and I won my first broadcasting job that day.

It wasn't all honey and roses from then on, however. The big opportunity I created for myself cost me financially. My secretarial job had paid me $120 a week. My first job in radio as an on-air reporter paid $89 a week, gross. I had to move back with my parents to cut costs. And that wasn't my only personal sacrifice.

Once I'd talked my way in, I had to become talented enough to stay there. That meant working harder and longer hours than anyone else on staff and using what little free time I had available to beef up my education. Immediately I enrolled in a night class at Harvard University in Cambridge for a course in writing, and on weekends I studied voice at Emerson College. At Harvard, one of my classmates was *American Journal* anchor Nancy Glass, who was at that time working on Boston's *PM Magazine* show. She, too, was shoring up her skills to ensure her future. She envisioned herself then as a successful national TV anchor, precisely where she is today.

As for me, my confidence rose with every new story I covered. After nine months on the job, I decided it was time to move on to television. I put some feelers out, but not for the job I reeled in—to my surprise.

"News desk!" I chirped as I answered the phone.

"Hello,"came the vaguely familiar voice. "I've been listening to you on my car radio. You've obviously learned a great deal since you left us."

I almost dropped the receiver. It was the general manager of the television station where I'd worked as a secretary. My ill-fated anchor audition was turning out not so ill-fated after all. It brought me to the attention of my former employer and made the man curious enough to listen to me on the radio. "Would you like to come back home?" he asked.

"As a secretary?" I quipped.

"No, this time you'll be working in News. You'll start as a reporter and we'll see where we go from there."

Where I went from there was the weekend anchor/producer position at the station, and later to a bigger job in another city.

Success was mine. Despite the odds against me, I had made the leap from secretary to TV anchor with only one stop as a radio reporter in between. And they said it couldn't be done.

"They" obviously didn't understand the power of personal leadership, which gives you the skills you need to overcome any kind of bad training and the confidence to turn disappointments into triumphs.

## IF YOU BELIEVE . . . YOU CAN SUCCEED

Leaders are visionaries who see tomorrow as clearly as others see today. "Far away there in the sunshine are my highest aspirations," wrote Louisa May Alcott. "I may not reach them, but I can look up and see their beauty, believe in them, and try to follow where they lead."

Alcott was a leader long before assertiveness became an

acceptable part of the feminine mystique. She wrote several novels in the 1800s, the best of which, of course, is *Little Women*. But becoming an author was not what her family wanted for Alcott. They envisioned her future differently than she did. They needed her income, so they believed she should be spending her life in servitude as a domestic. She proved them wrong by bucking the conventional wisdom of the day and penning a best seller, the income from which greatly changed the family's fortune. The world was saying no, but Alcott said yes to success.

As women, let's understand and accept the power of personal leadership and realize we do not have to be subservient to anyone. Successful women determine the exact direction they want their lives to take by examining all their options and selecting the path that is best for them. They steadfastly follow that path through to the end, where they accept full responsibility for the outcome. Along the way, these leaders rely heavily on self-confidence, courage, and a good self-image to keep them from steering off course. They use these attributes to fight off what I see as the six deadly demotivators that keep most women from finding success: fear, worry, doubt, negativity, guilt, and jealousy.

You'll never find successful women sitting around waiting for other people or events to make an impact on their lives. When they have their eyes on something they want, they get out there, shake the trees, beat the bushes, and *make* things happen. And so should we!

## WHEN LIFE GIVES YOU LEMONS, MAKE LEMONADE!

Storm warnings were up along the coast as the candidates converged upon the whaling city of New Bedford, Massachusetts, the historic place immortalized in the classic novel *Moby Dick.* The year was 1976 and I was a radio reporter. The U.S. presidential race was heating up. Soon, voters would cast their ballots in a primary to select the candidates they wanted to head up their respective tickets.

Offshore oil drilling in the formerly fish-rich New England waters was the magnet that drew the candidates to this spot. They were trying to score points with the mighty Fishermen's Union. And what a wonderful "photo opportunity" it would make on the nightly news: rugged candidates standing next to the manly Portuguese fishermen, heavily netted boats in the background. No matter that they had to dodge the seagulls screaming overhead as those sleek, feathered seafarers tried to bomb the newcomers with their white blobs of waste. It was a calculated risk but definitely worth the reward.

The male reporters at the radio station where I worked wasted no time deciding who was going to interview whom. Being the newcomer, I hovered at the outskirts of this meeting, hoping that as the impressive presidential pie was divided up, a piece would be left for me. But once the name of Sargent Shriver, of the famous Kennedy clan, was called out, I knew they had reached the bottom of the list. Hope was dimming. Could anyone else be left?

Only one name remained—obviously, a person with whom the experienced reporters couldn't be bothered. They laughed as they handed me my assignment.

"Here you go, Donna. You might want to brush up on peanut farming!"

As they walked down the hall, still chuckling, I looked down at the name: Jimmy Carter. The joke was obviously on them.

They were all headed to the fishing pier to jockey for position in an attempt to fight off the other media and get important "sound bites" from the candidates. Not wanting to follow the leaders, I made a few phone calls and found that Carter would be arriving at any moment at Fishermen's Hall for a meeting with the union boss. Afterward, he would push on to the pier.

Armed with my thin reporter's notepad, a pencil, a tape recorder, and my rain slicker, I rushed to Fishermen's Hall and stood waiting in the rain for my candidate to arrive. In minutes I spied the most unbelievable sight: what looked like an army of black ants crawling over the rooftops. They were, of course, Secret Service agents sent to protect this man who could be president. My stomach lurched as I realized the significance of what I had stumbled into that day. This man obviously had a real shot at the White House, for the Secret Service provided no other candidate that day with such a high level of security. This was definitely someone of great importance.

When the Secret Service determined that the coast was clear, except for a pesky female reporter who didn't know enough to come in out of the rain, they sent word to the motorcade to move in. I was awestruck by the unusual sight of several magnificent, sleek black limousines moving slowly down New Bedford's narrow, cobblestone streets. The middle limo pulled to a stop right in front of me. A Secret Service agent stood by my side as the car door opened and out stepped the friendliest man I had ever seen. My breath caught as the full wattage of his huge, toothy smile beamed at me. Talk about charisma, this man had more than his share.

Not knowing any better, I rushed up to Candidate Carter. "Sir, my name is Donna and I work for a local radio station. I have three quick questions to ask you." A hand clamped on my shoulder like a vise. It was a Secret Service agent who apparently decided I had gotten close enough.

Jimmy Carter looked me right in the eyes, grinned that toothy grin for which he's famous, and said in his slight drawl, "It's all right. I would love to answer your questions. However, I'm late for my appointment. Come along with me as I meet the union boss and then you and I will talk."

"Yes, sir," I said, filled with glee as I followed him.

As we were about to enter the union's small office, stale with the ghosts of a thousand cigarettes, the head union honcho came running out to meet Carter. He greeted him and then spotted me. With a rousing chorus of curses and expletives, he blocked the entrance and told me to get lost.

Over the man's shoulder, I watched as Jimmy Carter stopped dead in his tracks, turned, and looked at me standing outside the doorway. With a disgusted look on his face he said, "Excuse me, Donna, I need to talk to this man first, and then we'll have our interview." He spun on his heel and led the union boss into his own building. They shut the door. I don't know exactly what happened in there, but it had to be the shortest meeting on record. Both men exited the office and strode directly over to me. The union boss held his head down, his face flushed red with embarrassment.

I never learned who had been scheduled to take the seat of honor in Carter's limousine for the ride down to the pier. All I know is, that's where I ended up. After apologizing for the disrespect with which I had been treated, Carter told me we would ride around the city of New Bedford for as long as it took for me to get my one-on-one interview. I was stunned but recovered quickly, and I asked the questions my radio listeners wanted answered.

When we pulled up to the pier, I watched through the

smoky bullet-proof glass as the national media converged on us like a horde of vanquishers ready to plunder a new nation. In the midst of them, fighting for position, were the other reporters from my station. Unable to find me in the waiting throng, they decided I had fallen down on the job, and they were licking their chops at the idea of scooping up this interview. Belatedly, they realized Carter had become the choice assignment of the day.

Lights flickered on and cameras rolled as the media expected to see Carter emerge from the vehicle. Were they surprised when this pint-sized radio reporter, dressed in a hot-pink rain slicker and hugging her tape recorder, slipped out of the limo. I had just gotten the biggest interview of my young life—an exclusive personal interview with the man who would become the thirty-ninth president of the United States—an interview that even the veteran news hounds would envy.

*"Success is counted sweetest by those who ne'er succeed."*
—*Emily Dickinson*

# CHAPTER 2

# ... AND ENDS WITH SUCCESS

*"All of my life, I've always had the urge to do things better than anybody else."*

—*Babe Didrikson Zaharias*

Every time I think of success, the same picture forms in my mind. It's a portrait of a pint-sized Olympic athlete whose leadership and determination stunned the watching world in 1984.

Glued to our televisions sets, we held our breaths as tiny Mary Lou Retton vaulted her way to a gold medal as a gymnastics champion. It was a slice of life that could have gone either way. To snag the gold, Mary Lou had to score a perfect 10.0. There was no other way to do it; even a 9.9 wouldn't be enough. Fate had flipped the coin, but it was Mary Lou who would ultimately determine whether the coin landed heads up on success or tails up on failure.

It was now or never. This was the moment for which she

had trained her entire young life. Minutes before the competition, she ran to the sidelines for a last-minute pep talk
from her expressive and emotional coach Bela Karolyi. A
sideline microphone picked up their conversation. They
spoke only of success; failure was not an option. Karolyi
complimented Mary Lou on her achievements thus far and
then told her unequivocally that she was ready to win the
gold.

I watched as the huge, lumbering coach and the tiny,
graceful athlete put their heads together, giggling and
laughing like two school chums. Together, they visualized
the upcoming vault step by step. Mary Lou would run fast,
launch herself brilliantly from the springboard, reach new
heights, spin perfectly, and then nail the landing, smiling
triumphantly. They never mentioned the possibility of defeat, nor did they concern themselves with what the other
athletes were doing. They were both entirely focused on
what she had to do to win. There were no threats of "you'd
better go out there and do it right"; not a negative word
was uttered. They envisioned nothing but success.

Excitement had taken hold of this young champion.
Karolyi could barely hold her back. She was like a young
bull ready to charge. Her time was now and she knew it.
She was ready and equal to the challenge.

Finally, her name was called over the loudspeaker. Mary
Lou grinned broadly and bounced across the pavilion to
take her place. As she settled into her starting position, you
could actually see the determination reflected in her strong
face. She took a moment to calm and center herself. Then
with a rush of energy Mary Lou took off. I watched the
video in slow motion as she flexed her muscular body and
gritted her teeth. Not a trace of failure showed in that fabu-
lous face. She had shut out the rest of the world and was

focused entirely on springboarding her way to success.

Mary Lou raced to the springboard. Striking it perfectly, the young champion flew from the board as if she had the wings of Nike, the goddess of victory. She reached for the horse and propelled herself high into the air. Head over heels she tumbled perfectly, slicing the air as a diver cuts through the water. Then, solidly landing on both feet, she reached up to the heavens with arms opened and extended, grinning a smile which nearly broke her face in two. Mary Lou Retton was the picture of perfection.

The crowded auditorium broke into cheers. Bela was beside himself, nearly getting Mary Lou disqualified as, in a moment of passion, he began to run out to the floor, where he was not allowed.

Bela screamed on the sidelines, "Ten! Ten! Ten!" The crowd picked up the cheer, "Ten! Ten! Ten!" The judges' cards were raised, and they agreed: "10.0, 10.0, 10.0."

Pandemonium broke out in Pauley Pavilion as Mary Lou Retton vaulted her way into Olympic history. Winning more than the gold, she brought home a host of strong attributes, such as leadership, perseverance, courage, and determination, which she still carries with her today.

## LIKE MARY LOU, DO WHAT'S RIGHT FOR YOU

Success builds confidence as it smooths out our rough edges and removes any lingering self-doubts. It makes us stronger and better equipped to handle life and all the problems that come with it. Every challenge we successfully face brings out latent talents we never knew existed, especially when it's a lesson learned the hard and painful way.

I can taste the disappointment as if it happened yesterday. But it happened in 1979, when the news director at a

Rhode Island TV station pared down the list of candidates to fill the weekend anchor seat vacated by Meredith Vieira.

This is the same Meredith Vieira who later went on to fame as a national correspondent for CBS and the network's *West 57th* magazine show, and who subbed as news anchor on the CBS morning show before landing an impressive slot on *60 Minutes,* the top-rated TV news magazine of its time. After that she moved over to ABC's *Turning Point,* then became co-host of *The View* with Barbara Walters. Meredith—with the cute, perky nose, sultry dark looks, and a voice like silk. What a tough act to follow.

With the deck somewhat stacked against me, I had to be at my best. I pulled out all the stops in my personal appearance as well as in my professional skills, which I'd acquired at a rival station in the same type of role for which I was auditioning. Nervously, I sat at the anchor desk, watched for the red light to go on, then began.

"Not bad," I thought, pleased with my performance in completing an error-free audition. As soon as the lights dimmed in the studio, I made tracks for the news director's office to find out if I had made the grade. But he looked disappointed when I walked in the room, and I could feel my insides tightening.

He kept me standing for the longest time, not saying anything. Then he pushed his chair back, took a deep breath, and started to speak. My heart began to sink. He told me I had great potential, but it was potential that would probably never be realized because of the cruel joke nature had played on me. I was stunned. What in the world could he be talking about? What did he mean?

He went on to inform me that I lost the job "by a nose." Not just any nose, he told me, but *my* nose! He said that every time I turned my head, my nose "cast a giant shadow

on the set." It was just too big for a TV anchor. All my preparation, hard work, and determination meant nothing to this
man who couldn't see past my nose. Not stopping there,
he continued delivering one cruel, cutting remark after
another, each more personal and subjective than the one
before.

He managed to hit me everywhere it hurt by tapping
into every insecurity I ever possessed. My self-esteem,
which in those days was in perilously low supply, was taking a severe blow. Inwardly, I was reduced to tears at this
personal attack. Outwardly, I sat there passively smiling,
even thanking him for his advice like the good little girl I
was brought up to be. Can you believe that?

*If I had listened to that man, I never would have gotten to
where I am today.*

Don't get me wrong—it took me some time to pick up
the pieces of my shattered spirit after that devastating day.
But even in the face of this setback, I never stopped believing in myself. That news director did more than anger me
with his cruelty—he stirred up my resolve. I became determined to prove him wrong. I knew with certainty that no
matter what it took, I would make him eat his words. In
spite of his poor opinion of me, I became determined to
become a successful TV anchor. And I did.

## YOU NEED TO HAVE A PLAN

Becoming successful isn't like winning a lottery. We can't
leave it to luck. We achieve success with a well-thought-
out plan, hard work, and an investment in our goals. It's
essential to choose goals that require us to stretch ourselves
by exploring new ways of doing things. Once we believe
in ourselves and our goals, we gain strength and pick up
speed. We push obstacles away with amazing ease. Our

lives become less confused and less complicated when we allow ourselves the freedom to follow our own paths to success.

Our goals must also be meaningful or they're meaningless. By meaningful, I mean our goals must be worthy of our best efforts. For example, if I were to take a college communications course and get an A, it would not be meaningful. With twenty years' experience in broadcasting I could teach the class.

The successful completion of our goals takes us to our vision. Our vision is what we want most from our lives, where we want to end up, or, as author Stephen Covey puts it, what you want people to say about you when you die. It may not be what our families want for us or what our friends think is right for us. Instead, our vision is very personal and real, a powerful statement of who we are and what we plan to get out of life, in business as well as personally. It's important we know where we're headed before we take the first step on our journey, and it's essential we write it down, or we may get lost along the way. By writing down our plans, we make a subtle commitment to ourselves to follow through and find success. Goal-setting and finding the right vision are so critical to future success that I devote a chapter to each later in this book.

## HOW DO YOU DEFINE SUCCESS?

Start by defining what it will take to make you feel successful. Are you looking for a favorable outcome to a challenge? Do you desire fame, wealth, status, or power? Or do you simply want things to turn out as you had hoped they would? However you define success, you have the power to make it happen.

Next, take a good, hard look at yourself and assess your

strengths, talents, and abilities. This is not the time to be shy. Before you embark on the first of my ten steps to success, you need an honest appraisal of the attributes you bring to the table. Becoming successful means making the most out of what you've got while you actively work to develop other talents and effective leadership skills.

Can you often be heard saying, "Aw, it was nothing," after one of your successes? Well, say good-bye to that. The day of hiding our light under a bushel basket is over. We need to step out and be proud of our many achievements. We don't have to be obnoxious about heralding every success, but we do need to be straightforward about them and let people know what we've accomplished.

Articulating our achievements accomplishes two things. One: other people begin to see us in a brighter, new light. Two: even more important, we begin to see ourselves as successful people—women who want more out of life and know exactly what to do to get it. Complacency and settling for less become things of the past as we become motivated to do more with our lives.

I was speaking to a group of businesswomen recently and handed out a worksheet, which you'll find on the next page. It asks a woman to list all her current strengths, talents, and abilities. The group became very inspired, and rather than writing down their achievements, they began excitedly shouting them out. All except one woman, who sat dejectedly with her hands clasped and her head down.

I walked up to her and asked what was wrong. She picked her head up and with teary eyes said, "I have nothing." That shook me to my very core. Here sat a fifty-year-old woman who said she had no ability, strength, or talent —that throughout her fifty years she had accomplished nothing.

# LIST ALL YOUR TALENTS, STRENGTHS, AND ABILITIES

---

---

---

---

---

---

---

---

---

---

---

---

I sat down at her table, and with the help of other women in the group who knew her personally, we filled out her form. You should have seen what it looked like when we got done. This woman had totally taken her abilities for granted and underrated a vast number of her achievements. When she left the auditorium, she left as a new woman with a new, successful attitude.

Now I want you to fill out the worksheet on the opposite page. Think of everything you do, no matter how small. Don't leave anything out. Are you a good organizer? Are you an expert at wrinkle-free packing on those business trips? Put everything down.

After you complete your list, photocopy it from the book and pin the duplicate up in a private place or stow it away in your DayTimer or organizer. Refer to it only on one of those bad days when you don't feel good about yourself. Maybe somebody did or said something which makes you feel less of a person. Instead of being deeply affected by the remark, pull out your list and remind yourself of how special you are. You are strong and you can overcome. You have surmounted many problems in the past, and you can do so again. Use the list as a source of strength to bolster your self-esteem. Reflecting on all the things you do well eases the pain of laboring over what went wrong, and it puts you right back on the path to success.

## NEVER ACCEPT FAILURE AS AN OPTION

It's a simple psychological fact. If you believe you're going to fail, you probably will. Some of the worst advice my mother gave me was, "Don't expect to win. Then you'll be surprised and pleased when you finally do."

My well-intentioned mother never wanted me to feel

hurt and disappointed, but the flaw in her logic is obvious to me now. If you don't expect to win, then you won't do your best. However, once you refuse to accept failure as an option, you become committed to doing whatever it takes to be successful. And that includes accepting challenges.

Always challenge yourself. If you lose, you can still walk away with your head held high because you know you gave it your best shot. There is no sin in losing. The only sin is in not trying to the utmost of your abilities. You learn from every loss how to be better and more successful the next time. /

To me, at one point in my life, success came all wrapped up in a bright, shimmering gold statue: the Emmy® award that symbolizes the best in television news reporting. I knew, absolutely knew, that if I were ever to feel successful, I must be awarded that honor by my peers. Yet I was immobilized by fear of failure. You see, I had attempted the challenge once earlier in my career and been overlooked. I didn't want to fail again. I didn't want to feel worthless.

Back then, I had foolishly listened to a few of my counterparts, who lost no time in reaffirming my fears. "Why bother," they told me, "it's a waste of energy. It doesn't mean anything, anyway. You really haven't done anything worth submitting." What they were really saying was, "Don't rock the boat. If you excel, then they make us work harder. And you could become more successful and make more money than we do."

For a smart woman, I had been too thick to read between the lines. I believed them, and for the next several years stood by and watched other reporters and anchors scooping up the golden trophy. Finally, my desire for success outweighed my caution, fear, and self-doubt. I took a good, hard look at my work and at how far I'd come. I also went to the experts who had judged the Best News Anchor category before and asked them how to structure the entry to help ensure my success. In other words, I pulled out all the stops.

I won more than the Emmy that year. I won respect from my peers. More important, I found for the first time that I truly respected and valued myself. The Emmy was a validation. It said this woman has arrived; she has achieved success. But only after I received the prize did I realize my mistake in judgment.

Success comes from within. We shouldn't need golden statues to validate our worth. Just as we can't measure a man or a woman by what he or she possesses, we should never measure success by the number of trophies we accumulate.

## COMPARISON SHOPPING FOR SUCCESS

Another danger to our mental health and emotional well-being is measuring our success by continually comparing ourselves to others. It's a waste of time and energy that only fosters self-doubt and insecurity.

Whether it's a race to the finish line or just another day at the office, never be consumed by what the other gal is doing. Stop worrying about what she has that you don't. Instead, be like Mary Lou Retton—focus on yourself and your own abilities.

The only valid comparison you can ever make in life is to compare yourself now with the person you have the power to become. For years, I used the Joan Lukey method of measuring my success and came up short every time.

Joan was my yardstick, the woman I continually compared myself to. She was that girl in high school who could do absolutely everything better than anyone else. She always worked hard and never stopped achieving.

Do you have a Joan Lukey in your life? Even my mother thought she was great. "Why don't you dress up more, like Joan? She looks as if she just stepped out of a bandbox."

Joan was a cheerleader. I was a majorette. She became president of the student council. I was the vice-president. She made the Honor Society. I didn't. She was crowned Wareham's Junior Miss and went on to win the state title. I was crowned Miss Wareham but I lost the Miss Massachusetts title. Get the picture?

Although we were friendly, we were never true friends. There was a constant undercurrent of competition, at least on my part. In fact, I shied away from meeting her head-on in a challenge because I feared I would not be as successful as she.

Through the years, the quiet, unstated competition continued as she attended a prestigious college and became a lawyer for a respected firm in Boston. I took another road and became a television anchor.

Even when I began to write this book, I heard a little voice in the back of my head saying, "Well, this is something Joan has never done." It's funny how life works. Just moments after this fleeting comment zipped through my head, my telephone rang. It was Mom. She said, "Donna, I have some news. Guess who just had her first book published!" Well, it didn't take me three guesses to figure out that it was Joan.

It was on that day I finally gave up and decided once and for all to stop comparing my success to someone else's. Joan and I are both winners in life. We're just traveling down two different roads.

If you measure your success by constantly comparing

yourself to others, then the more people you know, the less likely you'll feel successful. Comparison shopping in the success market is one of the most destructive things women can do. Take my word for it, when we stop wasting time with worry, envy, and self-doubt, which are the natural by-products of using others to measure our success, we will become happier and more content—and more successful.

## DON'T GET TUNNEL VISION

Whether you're a power woman who's consumed with climbing the corporate ladder or a homemaker who can't see past her family to find her own success, you must broaden your outlook. Set your sights high and stop narrowing your focus. Look beyond what's in front of your eyes. Expand your vision of success to embrace many things in life. Never forget, the greatest limitations you will ever face are self-imposed.

When I was young and struggling financially, my limited definition of success was one day having enough money to afford a second refrigerator filled with extra food.

Things have changed for me over the years and so has my definition of success. Today it means:

- having a well-balanced life, full of highs and a modicum of lows;
- exercising my mind as well as my body;
- enjoying a loving, supportive partner, good social relationships, and strong family ties;
- being financially and mentally sound; and
- having great faith, an unshakable belief in myself, and a strong relationship with God.

To me, success also means taking chances, doing the work I love, and using courage to turn every obstacle into a story of success, no matter how great or small.

# SUCCESSFUL WOMEN
# GET WHAT THEY WANT

"How would you like to have breakfast tomorrow with General Colin Powell?" The question came from some well-heeled friends of mine who had to leave Chicago unexpectedly and would not be able to use their special invitation to Powell's Power Breakfast at the convention of the American Booksellers Association. Surprised by the offer, my husband and I scooped up the much-sought-after tickets to the important breakfast without hesitation.

Powell had breezed into the Windy City to whip up some excitement for his new book, which was just about to hit the nation's bookstores. We had heard that only the upper crust was being asked to break bread with the famous military man. We were delighted to have gotten the nod; however, the invitation came with a warning: "Be sure to arrive early to get a good seat." That advice proved to be an understatement.

My husband and I awoke before dawn the next morning and caught a cab for the convention center. We expected a bit of a wait even in the wee hours of the morn but were shocked to find the line circling the block outside the convention center. So much for a private soirée. More than a thousand people were standing in line before us.

We toyed with the idea of going back to the hotel, but instead resolutely stepped into line. I was determined to be successful in my quest to see the general up close and in person. No matter what the seating arrangements proved to be inside that packed auditorium, I was confident we could get close to Powell.

Disappointment struck as we entered the crowded auditorium. The first two-thirds of the room appeared full.

From the back third, where we were supposed to sit, the head table appeared no bigger than an ant farm. That's when I formulated a plan and launched an attack.

I asked my husband to sit down and told him I'd be right back. He began chatting with the other Powell fans and poured himself a glass of juice from the waiting carafe, but the glass never made it to his lips. Suddenly, I began hailing him from the middle of the auditorium, where I had moved as quickly as a cat and found two empty seats somewhat closer to the stage. I waved frantically until I caught his eye, and he soon figured out what was going on. Basically, I was using him as a placeholder as I kept on searching for closer seats.

Poor dear, he didn't even get to pour his juice this time before he was up and moving forward again, holding on to the next closest seats. We completed this ritual several times until we were about twenty seats from the general. It was then I spotted the table directly in front of him. From there, you could almost reach out and touch him. Amazingly, there sat four empty seats. It seems they were being saved for some big-time publishing executives who apparently decided they were powerful enough and didn't need to attend a Power Breakfast. Everybody knew the table was reserved for VIPs, so nobody dared approach.

Realizing that if you don't ask, you don't get, I summoned my courage and politely asked the trio sitting there if my husband and I could join them. "No problem," they said. "Welcome." We were delighted and took our seats quickly. After all, the only place closer than this would be in the general's lap. I breathed a sigh, looked up, and there was the general making eye contact with me. "Good morning. How are you?" he said to me with a twinkle in his eye. Apparently, he had witnessed my outrageous progress to the front of the room. "It's nice to finally *see* you, sir," I countered. The operative word here, of course, is *see*. In fact, the only person who couldn't see the general clearly from this close range was the person to my right, Dr. Ruth, the diminutive sex therapist who stands under five feet tall.

## BE DECISIVE

Successful women are not shy about doing what it takes to get what they want. They are decisive. Decisiveness is a leadership skill I learned not in the business world, but on the golf course.

Sports teach us a great deal about success because they are a microcosm of life. When we succeed on the course, court, track, or field, we carry the attributes learned from these achievements to our everyday lives. As we excel in our chosen sport, we start applying the principles of leadership in our home and at the office. Sports provide a nonthreatening way to learn some of life's hardest lessons, such as the endurance it takes to finish our race and the determination we need to hurdle any obstacle standing between us and success.

On one particular day I became so frustrated with the way I was playing that I wanted to toss my golf clubs into the nearest pond. I was the only woman in my foursome. My drive, which was always my strongest weapon, was letting me down. I began to get patronizing glances from two of the men in my group, which made me even angrier with myself.

Suddenly, my husband looked at me, smiled, and said, "Donna, it's all there. Don't worry. Just be decisive. Reach out and smack that ball the way you know you can."

Something clicked inside me when he said that, and as I started my swing I said to myself, "Be decisive!" Well, I hit that ball a ton. It looked as if it had been shot from a cannon instead of a golf club.

I outdistanced all the men with that super shot, but a greater victory was mine that day. The simple phrase *be decisive* said it all to me. To this day, when the old fears and insecurities start creeping back into my life, I step up to each challenge with courage and say to myself, "Be decisive!" and attack the new opportunity with all the gusto I can muster.

With effective personal leadership skills, all new challenges become great opportunities for success. As someone once told me, "Ten percent of life is what you're given, ninety percent of life is what you make out of it."

# CHAPTER 3

## STEP ONE:

## PLUNGE IN WITH A POSITIVE & COURAGEOUS ATTITUDE

*"I'm not afraid of storms, for I'm learning how to sail my ship."*

—Louisa May Alcott

It should have been a bright, shining moment, a first in a long line of success stories in this fledgling broadcaster's career. Instead, it turned out to be an embarrassment and a true-life lesson on why we need to approach every challenge with a positive and courageous attitude.

My assignment was to interview Jaques Cousteau at the prestigious Woods Hole Oceanographic Institution on Cape Cod in Massachusetts. The year was 1976. I was new to handling a microphone and eager to do a good job. My photographer was a grizzled news veteran who was beyond getting excited about anything short of covering a war. The thought of taking yet another young news reporter by the hand annoyed him, but that was his job.

If you've seen the movie *Up Close and Personal*, starring Michelle Pfeiffer and Robert Redford, you know just what I'm talking about. There I was, standing outside a sea of reporters, trying to stick my microphone over them and into the throng surrounding Cousteau. He couldn't have been harder to reach if he'd been submerged in a diving bell.

"Get in there!" yelled my photographer. He grabbed me by my arms, and pushing them tight against my body he lifted me off my feet and hurled me through the crush of reporters as if I were a crumpled pack of cigarettes. I landed about an arm's length from Cousteau. "Stick the mike in his face!" yelled my photographer, behaving in the same way as Redford's character, though looking nothing like him. I'm no Michelle Pfeiffer, but like her character, I got the job done.

As I made my way back to the station and put my film into the soup to be developed, I was proud and excited. In editing, I carefully cut the story together over and over until I got it right. My photographer came in, gave me a grunt of approval, and the piece was ready to air. The film was placed on one of two projectors used for the show. One was for news stories, the other for TV commercials.

As I sat at the anchor desk, I warmed with pride. This was a big moment in my life—a positive step forward that could only further my career. I wanted management to start thinking of me for the big stories. Making a mistake was not an option.

Finally, it was time. I took a deep breath as the red light blinking at the top of the camera signaled me to start. "Today, I met Jaques Cousteau," I began, and followed it with a lengthy build-up on the merits of this important maritime man, ending proudly with, "here's my report."

I couldn't believe what happened next.

Instead of Jaques Cousteau, up popped "Captain Crunch and the Crunchberry Beast." Someone had hit the wrong button and started the cereal commercial instead of my story. After thirty seconds of Captain Crunch's yo-ho-ho-ing, the camera came back on me. I looked like a deer startled by the headlights of an oncoming car. Thinking fast, I tried to determine what I could possibly do to save the situation. After a moment's hesitation, I softly chuckled, summoned up my courage, looked straight into the camera, and said, "Obviously, that is not Jaques Cousteau. That is Captain Crunch and the Crunchberry Beast." I kept smiling as I said, "We'll be right back," and the crew mercifully cut to a real commercial break.

I did get noticed that day by the management. However, instead of having a hearty laugh at my expense, they applauded me for handling a bad situation in a positive and courageous manner.

## IS THE CUP HALF EMPTY . . . OR HALF FULL?

Our attitudes have great power over the quality of our lives. They govern the way we think, feel, and act. Developed early in life, our attitudes are greatly influenced by the attitudes of those around us. Women who look forward to a great life filled with achievement possess a positive attitude, whereas women who focus only on the underbelly of life with all its warts reflect a negative attitude.

Environmental factors play a major role in determining how we approach life. If we're born into a family of overweight people who prefer snacking in front of the TV for endless hours as an alternative to exercise, chances are small we'll buck the trend and opt for a healthier, more positive

lifestyle. If the people who most influence us prefer col-
lecting a video library of horror flicks instead of finding
adventure in a good book, there will be no encouragement
for us to sharpen our skills and our intellect by slipping in
between the covers of a classic.

It takes effort to break away from the negative attitudes
that affect our lives daily, but if we truly want success we
need to learn how to filter out the negative messages that
assault us daily.

In the beginning, changing our attitude feels like an up-
hill climb. Many of us were reared on a steady diet of negative reinforcement by parents who used fear to motivate
us into being good little girls. It's not their fault. They didn't
know any better, because that's the way they were brought
up. Now that we're adults—free to make our own choices—
we don't have to play that game any more.

Negativity is a deadly demotivator. Changing your attitude is so important to your well-being, I detail several effective methods in Chapter 6 to assist you.

The moment we adopt a healthier attitude we become
stronger, and we grow stronger with each new challenge.
Soon, we become astounded that the girl whose best friends
were fear, failure, and self-doubt can do more than cope
with a complicated situation. She can excel.

## COURAGE SETS THE STAGE FOR SUCCESS

I learned that lesson time and again throughout my career. As a co-host for the television show *PM Magazine*, it
didn't take me long to realize that the best way to rise to
the top of my chosen profession was to accept the assignments others refused. Taking on what others found too dangerous or too difficult seemed easy at first, because in many

ways I was in a no-lose situation. If I did a good job, I was a hero. If I failed, "Well, at least she tried."

My courageous attitude has taken me on one exciting adventure after another, and it continues to do so. I've flown straight up to the sun and roared through the skies with the Thunderbirds in an F-16 jet, and I've soared while hanging out of a stunt helicopter high over a crowd of hundreds in the Wisconsin Dells.

I also survived my toughest assignment of all: cutting a triangular hole in eighteen inches of frozen lake, and with absolutely no scuba training, ice diving in weather forty degrees below zero. Putting my life on the line in this daredevil fashion was not something I wanted to do. Rather, it was something I pressured myself into, because if I didn't do it, the assignment would fall to my male co-host. In 1980, refusing assignments was not something women in broadcasting could afford to do. Many of us fought for years to be considered equal in the eyes of TV assignment editors across the nation. The ice-diving assignment was evidence of how far women reporters had come.

As my videographer and I approached the frozen lake, I racked my brain trying to think why I had ever agreed to such a dangerous stunt. Far from the warm waters of the Grand Cayman Islands, where breathtaking reefs and colorful water creatures are plentiful, this was Big Cedar Lake in Wisconsin, where, it appeared, hell had frozen over. It was like a scene from the movie *Grumpy Old Men*. A large expanse of white, the frozen lake was dotted with cars, trucks, vans, and tiny fishing shacks. It was hard to believe we could drive our van right onto the lake without cracking through the crusty top and plunging to our deaths.

Driving carefully by the fishing shacks, we found a group of men with chain saws cutting chunks out of the thick white ice. They smiled when they spotted us and waved us over. These were the ice divers preparing for the big event.

While my videographer went to greet them and set up his camera, I hopped in the back of our van and quickly slipped a skintight wetsuit over my bathing suit, which until that point had been under my thermal underwear. When I stepped out of the van I felt a blast of frigid air so raw it sucked the breath out of me. As I put on the borrowed wetboots and flippers, the ice was so cold my feet stuck to the frozen lake.

I could see nothing but clouds of frosty breath as the men shouted their instructions to me over the roar of the chain saw. They helped me fasten my weight belt. I felt as if I were wearing an anvil around my waist. It became difficult to stand. Then it got worse.

"Oppphhhh," I grunted, as the other ice divers heaved the heavy scuba tanks over my shoulder and onto my back. I sank to my knees, but one of the men caught me and started steering me to the black gaping hole in the ice—a raw, jagged mouth waiting hungrily to swallow up its next victim. Together we walked to the edge and sat down with our flippers paddling the top of the water. I looked into the hole for some sign of life, but nothing was there except inky blackness.

Then one of the men fastened a rope around my waist and attached it to another diver. It was supposed to be a safety precaution in case I failed to penetrate the gloom and find my way back to the small hole in the surface. But I found being snared by the rope frightening, and had visions of the other divers pulling me down deeper than I wanted to go. As I sat on the edge of the ice, I never felt more negative about anything in my life. I turned to tell my guide the truth—that I was not equal to the task and needed more instruction. Before I got the chance he pushed me into the water with a hearty, "Bye-bye, Donna!"

My head went underwater and I came up sputtering. My hands shaking with nervous tension, I wet my mouthpiece and slipped it back in but had trouble keeping my lips wrapped around it. I couldn't seem to suck in enough of the life-sustaining oxygen. To make matters worse, the mask made me feel claustrophobic. I started to panic. The guide sensed I was in trouble. He jumped in the water and held me. I looked up and saw everybody watching me. The camera was rolling. I didn't want to fail in front of so many people, so I decided a change of attitude was in order. Instead of fearing what I was about to do, I began looking at it as a great and wondrous adventure in which failure was not an option.

When you're putting your life on the line, you learn very quickly to approach every assignment or challenge with a positive and courageous attitude. You don't have a choice if you want to survive without injury. I was never more frightened and claustrophobic than when I slipped into the impenetrable darkness hidden under the bright crystal ice on that frosty December day. I had to quickly shed self-doubt and worry to keep a cool head and survive the experience.

I completed the dive safely that day. There wasn't much to see under the ice, but I'll never forget what I saw when I broke through the water after successfully finding my way back to the hole. My dive had attracted most of the people on the lake. They cheered me as they pulled me out of the water. They were proud that I had accomplished what few of them would try. But more important, I was proud I had found my courage to complete the dive.

# PUT A PREMIUM ON BEING POSITIVE

As in diving, keeping our heads above water is sometimes difficult when we're being swamped by negativity. We're often in too deep before we realize we're sinking fast.

Take the example of the woman who finds herself trapped in an abusive marriage. When she vowed to stick with her lawfully wedded husband through better or worse, she had no idea things would get this bad.

In her husband's eyes, she can't do anything right. He believes she's a failure and grabs every opportunity to tell her about it. She tries desperately to make the marriage work but she's coming unglued. People at work notice how negative she's becoming. It's a kind of ugly osmosis, as daily exposure to the demon seed results in her picking up his nasty habits. Sadly, she is the last person to realize she has changed. Finally, she reaches a point where she decides to do what's necessary to save herself. After all, none of us deserves to be treated badly. Admitting that she can no longer live such an unpleasant existence, she comes to see divorce as a viable though unfortunate option.

Sometimes we have to reach bottom before we can see our way out. Often our moment of brilliant clarity comes at the lowest point in our lives.

If it happens to you, don't despair. Use that time of reflection and courage wisely, and in addition to shedding an abusive husband, think about divorcing your negative "friends" as well. If married to an abusive alcoholic, divorce all the friends who enable and encourage your husband's bad behavior. Understand that they really aren't friends of yours. They certainly don't have your best interests at heart.

Actively work to distance yourself from all the people who consistently affect your life in an unhealthy way—all the naysayers who stand between you and success. Life becomes easier when you surround yourself with positive, successful people—true friends who want the best for you and don't waste time gossiping and complaining about life. Immediately, your success ratio will soar.

# YOU CAN'T DIVORCE YOUR MOM!

What do you do when it's your mother who is the Nelly Negative in your life? If it's not a phone call full of gossip about what the "kids" in the old neighborhood are doing, it's often a recap of every mistake you ever made. Mom means well, but after spending a lifetime dispensing advice and telling you what not to do, she is likely to dwell on the negatives in your relationship rather than the positives.

It's my belief that pointing out the negatives makes her feel more needed. When we are strong enough to stand on our own two feet, where does that leave her? Through the years, her role as Mom has diminished as we moved away, took a new job, or started a new family. She often feels the pain of separation more acutely than we do because she's the one left behind. And, if she's built her entire life around us to help make us successful, she may feel empty inside.

Many times, that's why the long-distance phone calls with Mom are filled with a litany of all the negatives in each of your lives. You never seem to discuss anything positive or upbeat. The two of you just keep rehashing the same old destructive things—all the miscues and mistakes of your past, with reminders of how she was there to help you out.

All these themes have absolutely no significance today, except in your mother's eyes.

Or perhaps your Nelly Negative has mastered the art of the gentle putdown without even realizing it. Let's say you are writing something important when the telephone rings. You pick it up. It's Mom. She asks, "What are you doing?" You say, "I'd like to talk, Mom, but I've got to finish this project." You are tense enough already because you're on deadline, and you can't seem to punch the keyboard fast enough.

Then Mom sweetly says, "Oh, I hope you don't get writer's block, dear."

Writer's block? Good grief! That thought never entered your mind—until now, that is. Thanks, Mom.

There are ways to improve your relationship and make it more constructive rather than destructive. Here's what my mom and I did. We worked together to break out of the old mold by playing attitude police with each other. When I get negative, she calls me on it. I do the same for her. We use the code phrase, "I love you but I'm all done talking now," and hang up the telephone without giving the other person the chance to reply. The "all done talking now" is a signal that the other person overstepped the boundaries we both set. At the same time that we're administering the hurt, we're applying the salve by saying, "I love you." Neither one of us takes offense, and we both work harder on the next call to rid ourselves of negativity.

After two weeks of some of the shortest telephone conversations in my life, we didn't have to do that any more, because together we formed a new, positive habit. The result is terrific. Our relationship is the best it's ever been, and her relationship with Dad has also improved as she uses her new-found technique on him.

# GOSSIPING DESTROYS A POSITIVE ATTITUDE

One of the most destructive forces to our positive well-being is spending an inordinate amount of time talking about people without their knowledge and savoring sensational tidbits about friends—and especially foes. In other words, gossiping.

I learned about the dangers of gossiping early in life. I was no more than ten years old when I fell "in love" with a boy from my elementary school. Alas, he did not share my feelings. No matter how hard I tried to get his attention, he always had his eyes focused on the little blonde girl who lived down the street. Unlike me, Laura was trim and athletic. She loved to play baseball and other "boy" games. She was popular and fun. My favorite pastime was reading in my room, or playing solitaire and word games. Being an only child, I had no sister or brother to draw me out of the safety of my upstairs room so I could experience life as my rival did.

I became desperate to get this boy's attention. So when my girlfriend approached me with a salacious little tidbit about Laura, I was more than ready to spread it around to anyone who would listen: sweet little Laura let the boys kiss her easily and often. I wanted it to be true so badly, I believed it instantly. But it wasn't true. It was a lie made up by a girl who was also jealous of Laura. She didn't want the danger of carrying the tall tale and figured I would make a great messenger. I'll never forget what happened because of it.

I went to the playground one day to meet the gang, which included both Laura and my beloved, unattainable boyfriend. When I walked through the gates, everything and everyone stopped. In unison, all my school buddies turned their heads and began staring at me. They all knew what I had done—that I had tried to hurt Laura's reputation. They adored their playmate, and at that moment they hated me. Led by the boy I cared so much for, they began jeering me and calling me names. I turned on my heels and ran home as fast as I could, up the back stairs and into the house for safety.

Still, I could not escape this angry crowd of children. They followed me home, hurling insults all the way. As I hid in my bed with the pillow over my head, I heard their tiny feet pounding up the long wooden staircase leading to the back door of our house.

My grandmother answered the door. They told her I was a liar and they hated me. I cried for days until I couldn't cry any more. Etched in my memory forever is the shame I felt. I still burn with embarrassment when I think about my mean-spirited attack. Even though I was a child, I should have known better.

Gossiping sacrifices integrity and character. People confide important things only to a person they trust and respect. If you are someone who gossips about everyone and everything, it becomes obvious to the people from whom you want admiration and respect that you're nothing more than a leaky bucket spilling puddles of information wherever you go. It won't take them long to catch on and decide to place their trust in someone more reliable.

Gossiping erodes our positive attitude by promoting negativity and wasting valuable time. The time we spend wondering who did what to whom could be put to better use—not to mention saving all the time it takes to cover one's tracks when people find out we've been gossiping about them. How many times have you had to run interference with one friend or another to undo the damage a piece of choice gossip has caused? That's time that could be put to better use finding success.

It takes courage and a positive attitude to change this nasty habit and forgo the momentary delight that comes from chewing on a tasty morsel of information about someone. You manage this change by simply monitoring your thoughts. Even if you're thinking about a gossipy, sensational piece of information, don't let it spill past your lips. And don't allow others to gossip in front of you.

By stemming the tide of negative input, you create a protective dam that keeps you from spilling over yourself. If someone else begins to share gossip with you, reach for your courage. Stop her immediately, and politely explain that you're not comfortable with this kind of conversation. Then change the subject to something more agreeable. When you do this, you are doing more than helping yourself. You are beginning to make the other person aware of what she's saying—and what you find unacceptable. From then on she will begin to think twice about gossiping.

## BEING POSITIVE IN BUSINESS

Maintaining a positive attitude is equally important in the business world. When we keep dwelling on the negative, thinking about what we can't accomplish, about what remains out there beyond our reach, and about who is doing what to whom, we are just spinning our wheels, wasting time, and shortchanging our success.

It's important we learn to handle the many things in the workplace that can drag us down—pettiness, avarice, unfairness, and cut-throat competition, to name a few. Instead of getting swept up in office politics or intrigue, we need to rise above all the unpleasantness and annoyances.

We are not responsible for the actions or attitudes of our coworkers, and we must never let their negative influences alter our positive attitude. If others succeed in dragging us down to their level, they don't have to work as hard to measure up to our standards. As a result, our work suffers and they look better by comparison.

Rising above negative or downright ugly situations is probably one of the more difficult things we may ever have to do on the job. It is so much easier not to resist and to go with the flow than it is to fight the current and swim upstream to a healthier, safer, more creative, and more pleasurable place. But the struggle to rise above is always worth it. Don't get caught in the undertow of a chaotic workplace, as I did.

By all outward appearances, I had it all. Viewers voted me the Number One Television News Anchor in my city. I was a woman who interviewed presidents, covered sensational trials, and talked with the stars. In everyone's eyes, I had the job of the century: spending a morning with Dustin Hoffman, an afternoon with Ollie North, an evening with the rock group Kiss, a day at the White House with President George Bush, and four days with Oprah Winfrey; visiting the yacht of TV mogul Ted Turner; and sharing the *Good Morning America* set with Charlie Gibson to tape a special story.

But unbeknownst to my viewers, I was riding in a work wagon whose wheels were about to fall off. As I let myself become engulfed, little by little, by all the misery and morale problems at work and the pressure of not letting it show, every avenue of my life became affected. I began to get migraine headaches, and I was told, "They're just a woman thing." My health began to fail—nothing major, just loads of medium-sized problems.

One day I talked with a doctor who was also a personal friend. "Want to get rid of your problems?" he said. "Then quit your job."

I took his advice and put out some feelers. What I reeled in astounded me. WHIO, a CBS affiliate and the number one television station in the Dayton, Ohio, market, not only wanted me to anchor for them but also offered me the largest and most lucrative contract of my life. I walked away from fifteen years at a station that seemingly did not value or respect me, and walked into the greatest deal of my life.

## NEVER SETTLE FOR LESS

It's important to like our jobs, because so much of our lives is spent at work. My years of experience have shown me that day-to-day life on the job becomes less problematic and more pleasurable when we and our employers share the same values and operate under the same code of business ethics. This is, of course, the ideal situation. Many situations in life are less than ideal.

Long before I entered the field of broadcasting, I had a horrible, compromising experience when I was an office worker for a small company. I was just covering up my typewriter to go home when the boss called. He explained he was at an important meeting and needed someone he could trust to take notes. I was flattered he trusted me with such a serious responsibility. I wasn't even his secretary. He said the meeting was of the utmost secrecy and I shouldn't tell anyone where I was going. All I had to do was hustle down to the local Holiday Inn and meet him in the bar.

At this point the warning bells should have been clanging loudly in my head, but I didn't hear a thing. I grabbed my notebook and headed out into the dark night. Money was tight and I could sure use the overtime pay.

When I arrived at the hotel I found my manager perched on a stool in deep conversation with a man seated next to him. He pulled up another stool and told me to sit down. Never bothering to introduce the other man, he offered me alcohol. I felt small and insignificant. I refused the drink and took out my notebook. Setting it on my knee, I awaited instructions. That's when the two men looked at me, then at each other, and began to laugh. My face reddened as I began to realize the joke was on me. There was no meeting. It was just a ruse to lure me to the bar. I felt cheap, even though I had done nothing wrong.

Offering one suggestive comment after another, they verbally toyed with me as if I were their plaything. Just how much of this am I supposed to take, I wondered, as I used my wits to fight off their attentions without making them angry. After all, one of these obnoxious men signed my weekly paychecks.

Finally, as they turned in unison to ask the bartender to freshen their drinks, I seized the opportunity to slip off my barstool. Mumbling a hurried good-bye, I made my get-away. I felt as if I were wearing a scarlet letter as I squeezed my way out of the room full of barflies—all of them check-ing me out with a knowing leer as if I were about to toss them a key to my hotel room and invite them up for a good time.

Returning to the office to finish tidying up my desk be-fore calling it quits, I found the building dark and empty. Everyone else had left work at 5:00 P.M.—it was then 8:30. Notebooks stowed away and typewriter covered, I reached for my coat and purse to leave for home.

Suddenly, I heard the front door slam. It startled me so, I froze on the spot. Moments later, my manager walked into my office. Staggering, he clutched the door frame with both hands. The cocktails I had seen him drink at the bar had apparently taken hold. One look at his face told me I was in big trouble.

His normal affable smile was now firmly plastered in a lopsided grin. He watched me for a while as if I were a bug under a microscope, and then, as I backed away, he lurched forward. Reaching out with his hands, he tried to grab me. I escaped and he tried again. If it weren't so frightening, it would have been laughable. I bumped into desks and knocked files onto the floor in my haste to get away. The office was in shambles. Papers were flying everywhere. Every time he put a hand on me, I managed to wrench free. I called for help but there was no one else in the building. I was frightened but felt sure I could keep him off balance because of his inebriated state.

Stumbling, he actually tipped a desk over on its side. As he tried to recover, I raced past him and made it out the door to safety. Only when I was safely locked inside my car with the motor running did I begin to cry. I couldn't believe this had happened to me.

How could I possibly return to work in a place like this, I thought. How could I face my boss tomorrow? What would he tell my coworkers about what had happened?

Quitting wasn't an option, for I needed the money. After returning home and pacing my tiny apartment numerous times, I tried to get some sleep, but my fretting mind kept Morpheus from me. Just after dawn, the telephone rang. It was my supervisor, who had decided to go to work early.

"What the hell happened in here last night? This place is a mess. It looks as if you had a party. Did you bring the beer in? I found an empty bottle on the floor. What's wrong with you? What the hell happened?"

I was young and frightened, and I didn't know what to tell him. I felt I needed this job and I didn't want to lose it. At first I tried to lie, to cover up for the manager so I wouldn't be fired. But when my supervisor told me how disappointed he was in me and how I had let him down, I knew I had to tell the truth, no matter what it cost me. This was the 1970s. Suing for sexual harassment was not an option in those days. I expected my supervisor to think I had come on to the manager, and he'd never believe my story. Saying good-bye to my short secretarial career, I took a deep breath and told him exactly what had happened. He listened but never said a word. I could feel his anger and was sure it was directed at me. I told him I probably would be forced to quit. He told me to report to work that day and we would work things out.

I was frightened as I walked through the doors of the small company, not knowing what to expect. My supervisor welcomed me with a broad smile and a black eye. He told me he had "discussed" the matter with our manager, informing him that I was a valued employee and shouldn't be treated like a call girl. I don't know how he got the black eye and didn't ask. I can only speculate that it was the price for defending my honor. I did, however, get an apology from the manager and a promise nothing like that would ever happen again at this company. And nothing ever did.

I kept that job only long enough to find another one—a better one. It became obvious my employer and I did not share the same value system. I had a strong work ethic, whereas he spent most of his afternoons and evenings socializing in bars. I wanted to work—he loved to play, trusting his supervisors to keep his business running in the black. He used his power inappropriately, by manipulating me with lies and deceit. His lack of integrity in dealing with

me was unacceptable. Furthermore, if he operated so un-
ethically with me, I couldn't imagine he'd treat others any
better—including his customers. I knew with certainty I
didn't want a future with that company.

# TAKE CHARGE OF YOUR LIFE

Competition is getting tougher out there as corporations
are forced to streamline, downsize, and become more tech-
nologically advanced to win a place in the global market.
Being positive in the workplace singles you out as a real
up-and-comer in any corporation. You quickly become a
standout, a person of real value to the company.

Positive employees add greatly to the success of any organization. When they get a bad break at work, they rise
above it quickly and move beyond it. When they're knocked
down, they bounce back on their own.

Instead of creating problems for the company, they solve
them. Ripe with grit, determination, and resilience, positive employees never fear showing their backbone. If they
get caught up in an ugly episode at work, they depersonal-
ize the situation. Not easily influenced, they refuse to associate with the corporate martyrs—the naysayers whose
chronic complaining hurts morale.

Positive employees find the silver lining in every black
cloud. Even if the company downsizes them out of a job,
they view their unexpected freedom as an opportunity for
even greater success. As many as one in five Americans
has been downsized or "re-engineered" out of a job.[1] Fate
has forced many of them to take a chance they couldn't
find the courage for until it became necessary. Mostly for
that reason, self-employment has grown an average of 12.7
percent annually, bringing the number of Americans in

---

1. Link Resources, New York, N.Y.

business for themselves to 22 million.[2] Of these, nearly 8 million are women. Women-owned businesses now employ one out of every four workers in the United States and are growing faster than the economy in general, bringing in $2.3 trillion annually in revenue.[3]

When one door closes, another one always opens, but we need the courage to get out there and find it. A courageous attitude is crucial to finding personal and professional success.

## CHALLENGES SPICE UP YOUR LIFE

Courage is bravely and confidently walking into a situation we know is fraught with obstacles and moving forward without slowing our step when facing overwhelming adversity. When approaching a risky situation, we refuse to allow fear to immobilize us. Our strong desire to fulfill our purpose drives us to overcome adversity and fear.

I was always kind of a wimp when it came to physical challenges, but that changed when I joined the staff of *PM Magazine*. When a camera is focused squarely on you and millions of people are watching your every move, it's amazing what you can accomplish. You become infused with a strange sort of energy. Ice diving was my first physical challenge. Shooting the rapids was my second.

With much trepidation, I adjusted the buckles on my bright orange life jacket and stepped forward for last-minute instructions. Everybody on the Peshtigo River in Wisconsin that day recognized me from television, and they were looking for me to take the lead and inspire them to

2. Link Resources, New York, N.Y.
3. *1996 Facts on Women-Owned Businesses,* National Foundation for Women Business Owners.

greatness. What they didn't know is that I had a great fear of being swallowed up by the massive wall of churning whitecaps and being pushed underwater down the river to a slow, agonizing death by drowning. I was not a happy camper.

The river was wild that day. The winter ice had melted in the high country, and the melt-off was rushing rapidly through the valley. There I was on a small rubber raft—not one of those big, family-sized ones. It was a tiny craft that soon would be racing past rocks and hurtling over whitecaps. My head started to pound. I felt that if I spilled over the side of the raft and plunged into the cold, raging river, I would never come up again. I wanted to cry. I wanted to run.

But somehow, I put on a brave face and started to counsel the three other thrill seekers in the group, who were also frightened. Sometimes if we pretend we're brave, real bravery begins. I knew I had to get outside myself and start focusing on the things I could control. I became educated very quickly about the proper use of all my equipment. I asked loads of questions about how to handle any situation that might arise.

Armed with knowledge, I stepped into the raft with the others and our guide. The first part of the journey was smooth and most enjoyable. But all too soon, we arrived at Volkswagen Rock. The locals call it that because it is as big as a Volkswagen car. Beyond that, I could see nothing but raging, white water. I felt sick. I knew I had to release tension, so I yelled. Not a woman's scream of fear, but a joyful yell, as if I were excited about being there. It was more like, "Yee-hah, let's go!"

Suddenly, I grew happy and excited, and I forced myself to look forward to the thrill. And what a thrill it became.

That rocky ride turned out to be one of the most important moments in my life. I felt superior, in control, and in charge. I had beaten the greatest force I had ever faced. No longer a weak sister, I had found real courage in the face of real danger.

I believe we must always challenge ourselves to stay sharp, physically as well as mentally. So don't shy away from a sticky situation. Dig deep inside, find your courage, and conquer your fears.

Soon after you apply this lesson to your life, people will begin to treat you differently. You will emerge from the pack as a leader. People will come to you asking for your advice in handling their problems. And the most astounding thing of all is that you will have the answers for them—answers you gleaned from your own personal struggle to be positive and courageous.

Every time I hear the Pointer sisters belt out their golden oldie, "I've Got a New Attitude," my toe starts tapping and my spirit soars. It never fails. The song moves me in a positive way, always reminding me of how far I've come—how my attitude has improved over the years.

Always remember, one woman's obstacle is another woman's challenge. It's all in the way she handles the cards she's been dealt.

# CHAPTER 4

# STEP TWO:
# STEP OUT WITH
# A STRONG SELF-IMAGE

*"No one can make you feel inferior without your consent."*
*—Eleanor Roosevelt*

Young people of today recognize him—because of the medicine he touts on TV—as a former athlete who suffers from painful arthritis. But to those of us who have been around a little longer, Joe Namath will always be the legendary football quarterback of the New York Jets, the Hall of Famer who, battered and often bruised, led his team to the Super Bowl more than once. No wonder he has arthritis.

When I was assigned to interview him back in 1977, he stood larger than life. Talk about a strong self-image, Namath radiated the same confident charm every time he appeared on television. His very strength and self-assurance were enough to make me nervous, for I was a young reporter, tentative, inexperienced, and totally devoid of any self-image of my own. I had less than a year of TV reporting experience under my belt.

"Go out to the airport and interview Broadway Joe!" barked my news director. He had just found out that Namath planned a public relations stop at a textile factory in New Bedford, Massachusetts, to glad-hand all the seamstresses and tailors responsible for stitching together his new line of clothing. I couldn't believe my luck as my first "superstar" interview fell right into my lap.

Before I headed out to the airport, I did some homework and studied up on this famous sports star. Little did I realize, however, that facts would play a small role in the upcoming question-and-answer session with this football star. In addition to planning a good offense, I should have been preparing a strong defense.

I stood on the tarmac as Namath's helicopter touched down, and I watched excitedly as my VIP debarked and casually strode over to where I was waiting. He appeared distant and aloof. It was obvious he could care less about me or my interview. His icy attitude eroded what little self-confidence I possessed. I felt inferior to his celebrity, frustrated by his obvious condescension, and unequal to the challenge of matching wits with this superstar. As I greeted Namath, my self-image slipped a notch. Instead of being assertive, I stood there looking to him for all the cues. I played his game instead of making him play mine. And he moved me around like a chess piece. As he grew even more uninterested, I felt the interview I had been so excited about slipping through my fingers.

Just when things seemed at their worst, the most amazing thing happened. As soon as my photographer turned on his camera, Broadway Joe turned on his charm. The transformation was amazing—as if Namath had slipped into an alter ego. In an instant he became a very likable guy, the friendly jock from TV we all knew and loved.

Beginning to feel somewhat better myself, I asked one question after another. He answered them all with that boyish grin for which he's famous. Then I ventured a final question and got a response that floored me.

"Do you have anything to add?" I asked.

"Yes," he said. "Here's something!"

With that, he grabbed me by my shoulders, pulled me close, and kissed me on the lips. It was a wet, sloppy, and disgusting invasion of my person. I was appalled and felt violated. Stunned, I tried to figure out my next move.

But when you lack a strong self-image, you are operating from a position of weakness. So instead of slugging him, or just politely informing him that I felt insulted and would like an apology, I did the unthinkable. I laughed out loud, out of sheer embarrassment. He looked me right in the eyes, threw back his head, and laughed, too.

Then as the photographer shut the camera down, Namath immediately ceased laughing and resumed the same icy demeanor with which he'd arrived. He turned his back on me and walked away. For him, this was all a public relations game. I suppose he thought I should have been flattered that he singled me out for the honor. But all I felt was cheap, used, and disgusted with myself for giving a totally inappropriate response to the situation.

When I look back now, I know exactly why I laughed. My self-esteem had already been jolted, so by the time he grabbed me I felt so inferior that I had ceased believing in myself; hence, my inappropriate response.

Can you imagine Namath getting away with doing something that outrageous to a woman reporter today? I am firmly convinced that had I possessed a strong self-image and taken control of the interview from the start instead of letting him control me, this unfortunate incident would not have happened. In my opinion, Namath was misreading the signals I was sending out. I was looking eager and hungry, even though my excitement wasn't about meeting the great football hero. I was just excited being a young reporter with my first big celebrity interview. I never took the time to see myself through another's eyes.

## LOOK BEYOND THE MIRROR

With the dawn of each new day comes another opportunity to view ourselves as others see us, but few of us rise to the challenge of looking beyond the mirror for a glimpse at our true reflection. Sluggish with sleep, we pad to the bathroom for our daily ablutions. In front of the mirror, we assess the superficial damage done by a restless night's sleep. Perhaps our reflection exposes wild hair that needs taming, unruly curls that should be smoothed into place, sleepy eyes that could sparkle with the addition of eyeliner and mascara, freshly scrubbed cheeks waiting for a hint of blush to add life, and naked lips hungry for a creamy gloss to make them appear fuller and more inviting.

To develop a healthy self-image, we need to move beyond the superficial. Instead of worrying about wrinkles, we should concentrate on inner qualities, inner strengths, and self-assuredness, becoming less concerned with how the world sees us and more concerned with how we see ourselves. Once we view ourselves—warts and all—as strong, capable women, the world can't help seeing us the same way. And the best thing is, we don't have to be rich, beautiful, or members of Mensa to step forward with a strong self-image. What we *do* need, however, is high self-esteem.

## PUMP UP YOUR SELF-ESTEEM

Good self-esteem is crucial to one's self-image. It's something we didn't have much control over in our early years. But there's no excuse now.

Self-esteem begins to develop soon after birth. It's a positive belief in ourselves, which in our formative years is influenced by how our parents, teachers, and friends treat us. Say, for example, you are a charming baby. People fuss over you and make you feel special; therefore, you begin life by feeling good about yourself. Your self-esteem soars.

Conversely, if you're treated as a difficult child or surrounded by inattentive people, you never feel any positive reinforcement coming your way, so your ability to filter out negativity or neglect is impaired. You get hit right where it hurts the most. As you begin to see yourself through the eyes of others, you don't feel good about what you see. When that happens, it's a blow to your self-esteem.

*High self-esteem gives us the courage and the strength to deal with life's most difficult situations. Poor self-esteem can worsen a bad situation and severely affect our self-image.*

When I was nine years old my self-esteem took a major hit. I was sent away to a children's hospital. The year was 1958, and hospitals functioned very differently than they do today. I was told I was going on the most wonderful vacation of my young life. The station wagon was packed chock-full with all my toys, clothes, and favorite things. But one thing kept haunting me: if this was going to be the best vacation of my life, why were Mummy and Daddy crying?

They had been told I had a blood disease and could die. The fact is, I had mononucleosis years before it became famous as the "kissing" disease. No, I really didn't engage in any kissing of boys at that tender year. Actually, I had contracted the measles, mumps, and chicken pox all within six weeks, so my immune system was on overload.

I spent six months in that awful hospital. Mom and Dad were allowed only Sunday afternoon visits for one hour. That's the way hospitals used to handle infectious diseases. Here I was, an only child far from home, ill, and erroneously believing my parents had abandoned me, or worse yet, didn't like me or love me anymore. I felt lost and alone. "What could I have possibly done to make Mom and Dad leave me here?" I wondered every day and lonely night of my forced incarceration.

Every day, it seemed, I sat in my bed and watched another child grow terribly ill or even die. Each new tragedy made me feel worse about my ability to survive this awful experience. Each time I wondered if I would be next. I learned a lot about fear in that place but not much about courage.

Unfortunately, I carried a lot of that extra baggage into adulthood, especially fear of the unknown, fear of change, and fear of living. After I left the hospital and tried to resume a normal life, all the fears, anxieties, and bad feelings accompanied me. Schoolkids shied away from me on the playground after hearing I had been ill enough to be hospitalized for such a long time. As they retreated, I became a loner. Although saddened by their reaction, I was also comforted by not being forced to be part of large groups of children who now frightened me with their unpredictability.

Every morning, I started the day the same way, sick to my stomach. Scared of life, I easily talked my parents into allowing me to stay home from school rather than face all the bad feelings engendered by that single, most devastating event of my life.

It took me years to realize that I was not responsible for all the garbage that went on in my past. The same is true for you. However, like me, you are responsible for ridding yourself of it now. Extra baggage, like the fear of change, weighs heavily on our self-esteem if we let it.

The key to feeling better about ourselves is to change our habits. A habit is something done often, and, therefore, done easily. It's one's usual mode of operation, like playing the victim, the "poor little me" syndrome. Nobody wants to be a victim, yet we slip into that negative role just because we're used to it. We do it too often and too easily, even when we know its potential for disaster

If this describes your standard mode of operation, you need to stop living in the shadows of low self-esteem. Instead, step out into the sun and add warmth to your world.

## YOU'VE GOT TO RESPECT YOURSELF

Learning how to respect yourself—for who you are and what you do—is important to improving your self-image. It means leading instead of following, understanding the importance of taking charge of your emotions and actions, and accepting responsibility for all the consequences of your decisions. When you respect yourself, you understand that mistakes can happen but failure is not an option. You can remain cool and confident in a crisis because you feel positive about yourself. Even as troubles batter you from every side, you still feel good inside.

Self-respect bolsters self-esteem, and together they form your self-image, which is as unique as your signature, as distinctive as your fingerprints. Once it's created, you strengthen it by successfully completing meaningful goals for yourself, operating with integrity, and refusing to allow other people to abuse you.

## FORM A POSITIVE MENTAL PICTURE OF YOU

A strong self-image is not conceit or an over-inflated ego. It is a positive mental picture of yourself that grows from respecting and recognizing your own abilities and talents. It's hearing "yes" when the world is singing "no." It's rising above your defeats and learning from your mistakes. It's about making the most out of what you have and not dwelling on what you don't.

A strong self-image is essential to becoming a success in the workplace or at home. If you need proof, look no further than Miss America 1995, Heather Whitestone. She's profoundly deaf, but her hearing loss proved no disability when she danced her way into our hearts to music only we could hear.

I interviewed Heather when she visited Dayton two months before her reign ended. She believes anything in life is possible with hard work and positive self-esteem. She learned that belief from her mother, who refused to allow Heather to be segregated from children with hearing. Her mother had endlessly researched all possibilities for her daughter, not just health-related, but educational as well. She enrolled her little girl in ballet class despite other parents' objections that a deaf child might spoil recitals.

Her mother never stopped believing that her deaf child would not only survive in a hearing world, but also thrive. That spirit of strength was carried on by the daughter, but not without its share of pain.

Heather laughs now at the memory of one of her first pageants on her journey to becoming Miss America. "I decided the best way to handle my deafness was to walk into the interview portion of the competition and try to fool the judges. But Donna, it turned out I was the fool. Instead of thinking I was deaf, the judges thought I was slow and stupid!"

It was on that day that Heather decided to be honest and to rely upon her strong self-image to get her through.

"The next interview was much different," she said. "I walked in and said, 'Hello, I'm Heather Whitestone and I'm deaf. I will be able to understand you but I need to read your lips, so I'd like you to speak slowly.'"

She didn't become Miss America that day either, but she became stronger for her next challenge.

At one point in her life, Heather entered four local Miss America preliminary pageants in five months. She became first runner-up to Miss Alabama two years in a row before she finally won the state title in 1994. Then and only then could she run for Miss America. Her self-image rose in the face of every defeat. Instead of being cowed by the competition, she was buoyed up by the realization she was one step closer to reaching her vision.

She learned more about being a victor from every defeat.

During her reign, Heather created a program to help young people develop strong self-images and become successful. It's called STARS, an acronym for *Success Through Action and Realization of your dreamS.*

We can all learn a lesson from this courageous young woman. She avoided a disability greater than hearing loss. Because of her strong self-image, Heather Whitestone would have been successful with or without her hearing.

# 5 ADJECTIVES I USE TO DESCRIBE MYSELF:

1. _____

2. _____

3. _____

4. _____

5. _____

# 5 ADJECTIVES I'D LIKE OTHERS TO USE TO DESCRIBE ME:

1. _____

2. _____

3. _____

4. _____

5. _____

But a poor self-image would have kept her from succeeding even with the best hearing. Low self-esteem, in many cases, is the greatest disability of all.

It's bad enough when we let our limitations get in our way, but worse still when we allow other people's negative perceptions to affect our lives. As Heather knows from personal experience, "Anything is possible. Regardless of our physical abilities, our race, ethnicity, or gender, or even our social or economic background, we can achieve our dreams if we believe in them and our capability to make them come true."

Like Heather, you need to feel good about yourself. Let's find out if you have the right stuff to become a strong, successful woman.

## HOW DO YOU SEE YOURSELF?

It's important to not only identify the self-image you currently have, but also decide what you *want* it to be.

Look at the worksheet on the opposite page and list the five adjectives that best describe you. Be truthful and honest. Don't think too deeply on this one. Just grab the words off the top of your head. Don't ask for advice or help from anyone. Sit there until you come up with the top five.

Next, move to the second half of the exercise. Choose the top five powerful adjectives that you would like to have other people use to describe you. Go ahead, pull out all the stops. This is no time to be coy.

When you are finished, compare the lists. Is there any difference between the way you see yourself and the way you want to be seen?

The first time I tried this exercise it was not only enlightening but also painful. The first half of the lesson revealed my passive nature—the side of me everyone else walked on, while the second list showed I longed to be assertive, nobody's patsy. The differences between my two lists were astounding, forcing me to realize I had subbasement-level self-esteem. How about you?

A poor self-image creates an invisible barrier between us and the rest of the world. It becomes a glass ceiling far more difficult to crack than the one in the office.

When we're burdened by a weak self-image, color drains from our lives. Everything we touch becomes tainted, because each decision we make is created from a position of weakness rather than strength. It is filtered through a network of fear, doubt, and self-loathing. We don't ever ask for what we need, because we don't feel we deserve it, and we're right! If we think we're not worth much, then what's our opinion worth to others? How can anyone value our opinions and beliefs if we don't value them ourselves? We come to expect less out of life, and—guess what?—that's exactly what we get.

Ask my girlfriend Yvonne a question and she'll quickly respond, "I don't know," even before she's had time to consider the answer. It's automatic, and it's a bad habit. She's had this habit since she was a little girl. Today, she is an adult and has a husband, three children, and a poor self-image. She desperately wants to change. Yvonne is smart, knowledgeable, funny, and clever. The only problem is, she doesn't know it.

Even when Yvonne knows the answer, she doesn't have the belief in herself to state her opinion to others. She feels her opinion has no merit because she doesn't respect herself.

How about you? Do you use "I don't know" as a way of putting people off and not accepting responsibility for your actions? Sometimes it's easier to say "I don't know" than to accept the consequences that may come with saying exactly what's on your mind.

Accepting responsibility for the consequences of our decisions and actions is one of the fastest ways to create a strong self-image. Our self-image swells once we stop shirking responsibility. Taking control of our own lives makes us feel good about ourselves. After all, we're not children anymore. We no longer live in an environment over which we have little or no control.

When I was a young girl, Mom and Dad called all the shots. I grew up and left home. I lived alone. I wanted people to like me, so I let them call the shots. I was content just pleasing everybody but myself. I matured, but unfortunately my self-image didn't. Emotionally, I was still a teenager.

Conservatively reared as a small-town girl, I feared big-city life as much as making my own choices and decisions. Then, in 1984, I married a strongly opinionated man who called all the shots. I finally got fed up, walked away from that destructive relationship, and began making my own decisions and accepting responsibility for the consequences.

It was then that I really began to live. My self-respect and self-esteem soared, propelling my self-image to startling new heights. Instead of being afraid of making decisions, I became eager to express my opinions.

## AVOIDING DECISIONS NEGATIVELY AFFECTS SELF-IMAGE

Some women feel they can skirt the whole decision-making process by avoidance. They remain mute rather than express their beliefs or convictions, because they fear exposing themselves. However, by not saying anything, they are still communicating a strong message. They are saying,

"How I feel has no merit. Go ahead, you're more important than I am. You make the decision. After all, I don't
want to be responsible for making a mistake."

There's a serious flaw in this logic. By refusing to make
a decision when one is called for, they have, in reality, made
a decision—the decision to do nothing. They have lost an
opportunity to gain respect in the eyes of others. More important, they lose respect for themselves, the respect that's
crucial to maintaining a strong self-image.

A woman who continually avoids making decisions is
ripe for an abusive relationship. If we forgo the challenge
of making important decisions about our lives, there are
people out there eagerly awaiting the chance to do it for
us.

They are the users who thrive on controlling other
people's destinies. At first we may be relieved because
they've lifted the heavy weight of decision-making off our
shoulders. Little by little, we begin handing over bits of
our self-respect until there's precious little left. Soon, we
lose our will to fight for what we desire most in this world,
and we don't like what we see in the mirror. Users sap all
the life out of us, if we let them. But each of us has the
power to keep this from happening.

## IT'S YOUR DECISION!

Start making good decisions today. If the thought of accepting responsibility for them frightens you, start small.
When people ask you where you want to go to dinner, don't
say, "Oh, any place you want is fine." Be decisive and take
control. Choose your favorite place.

If we can't make a simple decision about dinner, how
can we trust ourselves with the big decisions in life? We
have to learn to make decisions based on our desires and

the facts as we know them, not because of someone else's whims or because we're being bullied into doing something we really don't want to do.

The first step in making sound decisions is to gather all the necessary facts and information. Take the time you need to make an educated choice. Don't be pushed into hasty action due to someone else's demands.

Let's say your children are really bugging you today. "Mommy, I want to eat supper over at Kay's tonight. Can I, please? She's on the phone. I have to know now, Mommy."

You would really like to think this through but your daughter's pressing you. Kay is very nice, but she and her siblings watch a little too much MTV, and you feel your daughter is not quite ready for all that stimulation. But your daughter is employing a strategy that has worked for her in the past: wear Mom down so she'll say yes just to end the whining.

Try something different the next time this happens to you. Say very gently and firmly, "Susan, I'm very busy, but if you need an answer right now, that answer is no. If you're willing to wait and let me think it over, I may change my mind. However, I'm not making any promises."

This is a good strategy, and it works in business as well as in the home. "If you ask me now, the answer is no, but I'd really like to think it over."

## "OOPS, I MADE A MISTAKE"

The woman who digs in, makes her own informed decisions, and accepts responsibility for them, right or wrong, earns admiration from others as well as self-respect. But what if, heaven forbid, we make a wrong decision? It happens more times than we would like it to. Every time we make a decision, we stick our necks out.

You're sitting out there alone on a shaky branch waiting for somebody with a chain saw to come by. It's risk versus reward.

From the branch where I'm sitting, I find the potential reward of earning the admiration of others and increasing my own self-respect much greater than any risk I take from making a bad decision.

What do you do if the worst happens? Apologize, fix the situation if you can, and quickly move on. Don't dwell on mistakes. Just learn from them. Don't ever be ashamed to say, "I'm sorry, I made a mistake." Apologizing does take courage, but it's the kind of courage admired and respected by others. It's good fuel to feed your self-image.

There is only one time we should never apologize when making a decision, and that's *before* we make it. How many times have you said, "I'm really sorry, but I think we should do it this way"?

Asking for permission is a cowardly thing to do. Women who fear being wrong always ask for permission before they make a decision. That way they get someone else to affirm that what they've decided is, indeed, the way to go. So the other person takes the risk, not the woman who made the decision.

But look at what she's sacrificed. In one brief action, she transferred to another person her risk, her ability to choose, and her considerable power.

Does this sound like you?

Say, for example, you're writing a big report for the boss. You decide the company needs to make a change to improve business, and you have a great idea for how to accomplish it. You want to put your brainstorm in the report, but you're not sure the boss will receive your idea in the good spirit with which it's being given. So you go to your supervisor, or to another coworker, or even to your husband, and essentially ask for permission to put your idea into the report by saying, "What do you think about this?" By uttering that one seemingly simple question, you have compromised your intelligence and transferred your power of choice to another person. The other person now takes the risk, not you. If the decision turns out to be a bad one or the boss hates your idea or your report, you can now shift the blame. Isn't that what you really wanted to do in the first place?

Part of the problem of not being able to make strong, independent decisions comes from childhood. As young women, many of us were raised on a steady diet of Mom and Dad asking, "Are you sure you want to do that, honey?" Yet our male siblings were often told, "Just go out there and do it. Get the job done."

As we grow into womanhood, we carry that baggage with us and often over-intellectualize every situation. It's a habit and a bad one. While the young men were coaxed to approach every situation with courage and confidence, some of us were taught to hold back and apply caution rather than confidence. If this applies to you, it's time to toughen up.

## WHEN THE GOING GETS TOUGH . . . DIG IN

*Stop* eroding your self-respect by asking others for permission to do what's right for you.

*Stop* handing over your power to someone with a personal agenda that doesn't include looking out for your best interests.

*Stop* believing that what you think or feel is less important than what everyone else thinks.

## YOU'RE IN CHARGE

You alone are responsible for creating your self-image. No one else can do it for you. You have to make it happen. If it were easy, everybody would have a great self-image.

It's time to stop finger-pointing and blaming everyone else for the problems that plague us. The day is over when we nursed real or imagined hurts forever. Our self-image strengthens when we stand squarely on our own two feet.

You know you've arrived when you make one of the biggest or most controversial mistakes of your life and you still feel good about yourself. Even in the middle of the mess you accidentally created, you still see yourself as a strong person, but one who just happened to make a mistake. Your strong self-image will see you through.

And when you've done a terrific job, be the first one to applaud your actions. If you're going to take the blame for the bad, then don't hesitate to feel pride for a job well done.

Your strong self-image is one of your most valuable possessions. It can get you through a lot of tough spots. So don't tarnish it by doing something that makes you feel bad about yourself. Only you have the power to change your self-image.

## PLEASING PEOPLE COMES NATURALLY

Few things are more unbecoming in life and harmful to our self-image than being a pandering people-pleaser. It's nice to want to make all our acquaintances feel happy, but there's a limit. Their happiness is not something we can control. Happiness comes from within. We lose respect for ourselves when we trade off our beliefs and convictions to get another person to like us.

Remember this essential point: it's far more important to have people respect you than it is to have them like you. Personally, I would rather have somebody's admiration than their good cheer. Many of us have trouble swallowing this concept because we've been raised to believe that pleasing people is one of our most important duties. Well, I'm here to tell you that sacrificing what's important and vital to oneself just to become a people-pleaser doesn't work.

Take the example of the perfect wife who works hard to make a nice home for her husband and family. She's eager to please and always drops her plans at a moment's notice when her husband announces he has other plans. She lives for him and her children. She is dependent upon his moods and upon his money. When he's not happy, the whole house suffers. So she works to keep him happy. Then one day he knocks the pins out from under her. He comes home and announces he doesn't love her any more. He's found someone else. A woman in his office. A real go-getter who knows how to get what she wants. An independent woman whom he respects and admires. The wife is left behind wondering what went wrong. How could this have happened when she sacrificed everything—including her self-respect—to give him exactly what he wanted?

When we have a strong self-image, pleasing people happens naturally. We don't have to work at it or sacrifice our beliefs.

# LEARN FROM OTHER STRONG WOMEN

No matter how strong our self-image is, every now and then we run across a woman who has raised self-image to an art form—a human dynamo who knows exactly what she wants and understands how to get things done. She's a true success and a woman we'd love to emulate.

So why not emulate her? Learn from her. Strong women have much to teach us. Just watch. Observe how she takes charge, takes ownership, and gets results. Don't waste time being jealous of who she is and what she has. Find out more about her. Ask questions. What does she know about being positive and strong that you need to know? How far has she come and how tough was her journey to make her image of herself so strong and worthy of your respect? What can she teach you?

One thing I'd be willing to bet on is that she really respects and loves herself—and she's proud of it. Many of us growing up were taught that self-love is wrong. It's conceit, it's ego. But it's not.

In the Bible, a law expert asks Jesus if God wants us to "love your neighbor as yourself." Jesus says, "You have answered correctly."[4] Why would God make that comparison if God didn't expect you to value and esteem yourself?

## SOMETIMES YOU NEED TO FAKE IT TO MAKE IT

You might be shocked to hear this next piece of information, but pretense is a major part of creating a good self-image. Sometimes we need to fake it until we make it. We need to see ourselves as strong and successful women while we work on increasing our self-esteem and self-respect to make them real—as long as we are careful to not wear the mask too long.

It's acceptable to put up a strong facade while actively working on doing what it takes to truly feel better about ourselves and our abilities, but we aren't able to keep up the act forever. And we shouldn't want to even if we could.

---

4. Luke 10:27-28 (NIV).

Freedom from pretense is an exhilarating and liberating experience, whereas a life filled with phoniness ultimately caves in like a ramshackle clamshack on a Cape Cod beach during a strong gale. In time, stress cracks the veneer of even the most skillful poser, exposing her true character. People spot her as a phony. Then where will she be? Her word will mean nothing, because it's based on lies. How will she feel about herself then?

A little pretense goes a long way. In the early days of my career as a TV anchor, there were times I felt insecure about myself and my abilities. So I would sit before the studio camera, facing hundreds of thousands of viewers on live television, and pretend to be Barbara Walters or Diane Sawyer. Usually the pretense lasted only as long as it took me to complete the first story. That's about how long it took me to relax, dig deep inside, and bring out the good feelings buried within me. With every successful performance I grew, and soon I didn't need to pretend any more. It was much more fun being me.

## SEE YOURSELF AS YOU WANT TO BE SEEN BY OTHERS

My husband recently told me a wonderful story about a young prince who couldn't walk. He asked his father to build him a statue, only instead of being seated, the child insisted his image stand erect and without support. His father acceded to the child's request but asked why. The child answered, "That is the way I see myself, tall and proud."

For years, the child looked at the image of himself in the garden and strove to emulate it. By the time he reached adulthood, as the story goes, he had learned how to stand erect, without support. The young prince had created a strong self-image built initially on pretense, but with hard work he made it happen.

You can make it happen for you, too.

# CHAPTER 5

## STEP THREE:
## LENGTHEN YOUR STRIDE WITH SELF-MOTIVATION & WILLINGNESS TO CHANGE

*"Opportunities are usually disguised as hard work so most people don't recognize them."*

—Ann Landers

Sometimes we just have to make something happen. When it comes to being a reporter I have never been a shrinking violet. I can't sit around and wait for the big stories to be handed to me. The lesson is one that works for others.

We need to be highly motivated and willing to fight for what we want. We don't get anywhere in life by resting on our laurels or our posteriors. Getting out there and making things happen is essential to success. Such was the case in my determination to cover the sensational story of Susan Smith, the woman now reviled as the World's Worst Mother.

Smith became infamous for drowning her two small boys in a car that she pushed into a cold, black South Carolina lake. We had all sat and watched our TV screens as this seemingly grieving mother moaned and shed crocodile tears over the loss of her two beautiful sons, who she claimed had been taken by an unknown carjacker.

The nation waited with bated breath as the search expanded for the boys and the alleged kidnapper. Eventually, Smith began to buckle under the horrific weight of the ordeal, and she broke down and admitted her guilt. It was she who had put the boys in the car, she who had pushed the car down a boat ramp into the dark and icy lake, she who had killed her own children.

After holding the nation's heart hostage for weeks, she was about to be arraigned for her heinous crime in the small southern town of Union. I was highly motivated to cover this incredible story, but I sat hundreds of miles away in Dayton, Ohio. So I thought hard and came up with a cost-effective plan to cover the arraignment live by satellite, renting local on-site equipment. I pitched the idea to my boss, and within forty-eight hours I was on a plane for the Carolinas. I was scheduled to arrive only an hour and a half before my first live appearance, or, as TV jargon would put it, a live shot.

A lot of work and running around goes into each television live shot. Every minute the viewer sees on the air requires hours of work behind the scenes. But when you are highly motivated you care little about the workload. You just do what needs to be done as quickly and as efficiently as possible.

In this case, I was hampered by some bad information.

My assignment desk in Dayton had instructed me to go directly to the jail where Smith was being held instead of to the courthouse in Union. That sounded good to me, because it was closer to the airport and I was running late.

I knew I was in trouble as soon as I drove up to the jail in my rented car. All was quiet, too quiet—not a TV camera or satellite truck in sight.

"She's gone, lady . . . left for the courthouse in Union a couple of hours ago," said one of the jailers in reply to my question concerning Smith's whereabouts. "Took all the media with her," he added with a smile.

"All but one," I replied ruefully as I explained to him that I had only one hour left to make my time slot for the live shot.

"Then you got problems, lady. Union's an hour's drive from here. You can't possibly make it by then."

After a hasty good-bye and a hearty thanks for the information and the directions, I put the pedal to the metal and sped off for Union.

My head started to pound as I hot-footed it to the biggest story of the year, now slipping through my fingers like sand through an hourglass. Even if luck was with me, I would have only fifteen minutes after my arrival to gather the latest information, find my satellite truck and videographer, and set up for my live shot.

Union looked like a town under siege by the frenzied media. All the main streets were shut down by dozens of satellite trucks, and traffic everywhere else was impaired, including cellular traffic. In fact, the morning of the arraignment, the entire cellular phone system went on overload and no one could get a cellular call in or out of Union. Still, I needed a phone, a land-line. But not even a pay phone was in sight. Desperate to connect with the station back in

Dayton, I visited the tiny shop of a shoe repairman and sweet-talked him into letting me set up a makeshift office in his back room. Then I went to search for my local crew. I assumed they would be located near the side entrance of the courthouse to which Smith would be driven for her arraignment, the best vantage point to catch all the action. They were. In fact, they were set up, ready to go, and anxiously looking for me.

"You're not going to make it," they warned.

"Don't bet against me," I replied. "I didn't come this far for nothing."

I felt time closing in on me. I had only three minutes to find out what was going on behind me and report it to the viewing public in Dayton.

I found out what I could. Smith was being held somewhere else and had not yet entered the courthouse. I would use that information and describe the mood of the community. Centering myself in front of the courthouse and running a quick hand through my hair to snag any recalcitrant curls, I grabbed the microphone as my director, seated in the satellite truck, spoke to me through my earpiece.

"Thirty seconds," he said.

I took a deep, cleansing breath and let it out slowly. What happened next was amazing.

Just as the anchor in Dayton was introducing me and explaining my presence in Union, I heard a rumble behind me. Susan Smith was on her way into the courthouse amid jeers of "baby killer" from an angry crowd. I turned and over my shoulder saw a scene filled with raw emotion, as people who felt betrayed by Smith's deception heaped verbal abuse on her. I began to describe the dramatic event to the viewers waiting in their Dayton homes. Luck had handed me my live shot. The drama of the moment, the scurrying behind me as Smith entered the courthouse, made what we call in the business "good TV."

I got the story, despite all the stumbling blocks, because I was extremely self-motivated for success and refused to accept failure as an option. First I'd been told I wouldn't be able to go to Union. Next I was sent to the wrong place, where I was told not to hurry to the right place because I wouldn't arrive in time anyway. Then I was told by my TV crew that I wasn't going to make my time slot. They were standing by to cancel it, to give it to someone else. Each one of those naysayers obviously confused me with someone who lacked the necessary self-motivation for success.

# SHIFT INTO GEAR
# WITHOUT STALLING

Motivation is an inner need which forces us into action. It's usually caused by an unrest or uneasiness in our present situation. Everybody gets motivated to do something at one time or another, but the key to success is to be self-motivating all of the time.

Once you've met your basic needs—food, shelter, clothing, and safety—what is it that motivates you? Do you want a new job because you're dissatisfied with your present one? Or is your dissatisfaction based on something as simple as wanting only to contribute more to your community, friendships, or marriage? How about a larger house, a better job, enrolling your child in a private school? Whatever it is, your need must be strong if it is to motivate you.

Take a minute and think about the forces that motivate you. What need or desire do you have that makes you itchy enough to move forward to scratch it?

On the next page, write your top five motivators, so you get a clear picture of exactly what your inner needs are.

# WHAT MOTIVATES YOU?

1. _____

2. _____

3. _____

4. _____

5. _____

Do you want to beef up your self-image or become more fulfilled, more socially accepted, more successful? Do you want to have more power and control, become a more important person, or make a lot of money?

Something on your list will be strong enough to make your motivational juices flow and push you into action. Something will represent a need so powerful you will be willing to shed your old familiar habits for the unknown. Self-motivation happens when you're willing to trade off your energy and skills to get whatever it is you need.

# TRIGGERING MOTIVATION IS A FULL-TIME JOB

Don't be like the gal I call "Short-Time Susie." When she sees something she wants, she works hard to get it, but her one big failing in life is she can't motivate herself for long periods of time. Her inspirations come in short bursts. She gets motivated just long enough to go out and win what she desires at that moment. Once Susie accomplishes the task and satisfies her appetite, her motivation wanes and it's back to square one, just sitting around and waiting for life to come to her.

Are you like "Short-Time Susie"?

- Does it take a crisis, or a need so strong you no longer can ignore it, to send you into action?
- Do you appear to have boundless energy and initiative but never seem to get things done?
- Do you have conflicting desires that keep you from motivating yourself?
- Are you torn between being yourself and being accepted by others?
- Do you shy away from challenge and achievement because you tried it once and failed?

- And do you wonder why, once motivated, you can't
  stay motivated so you get even more out of life?

Unfortunately, too many women feel more comfortable sitting around complaining about what they don't have. They have lost interest in rising above reality.

Comfort breeds laziness. The longer they sit, the more complacent they become, until all of a sudden what they wanted most is no longer worth the fight. Laziness sweeps over them like an old friend, enveloping them like a soft, warm afghan on a comfy old chaise. But it's a warmth that can freeze them into immobility and keep them from moving ahead.

Some women appear to have no cares or worries, a never-ending bank account, and an unlimited supply of Godiva chocolates to devour as they sit watching one classic movie after another. They vicariously live the heroine's life while their own lives slip away unnoticed with every click of the channel changer. Laziness may have some appeal, but self-motivation and a willingness to change are what bring us satisfaction and achievement.

## WISHING DOESN'T MAKE IT SO

Successful women don't sit around and wish for better circumstances. They are actualizers who can go out and make things happen. I won't lie to you—motivating yourself is not the easiest thing you'll ever do. But if you start stirring your stumps to get moving and get motivated, I promise you a satisfying life filled with achievement.

Sometimes, it means shedding an old attitude. Other times, it could be altering your appearance. I've done both, more times than I can count.

I don't know if blondes have more fun, but when I was starting out they definitely got more work in the television news industry. Take it from this brunette-born anchor, if I hadn't had a willingness to change and the motivation to make that happen, my career might have stopped before it really got rolling.

I had just landed my first broadcast job reporting and anchoring weekend television news at WTEV in Providence, Rhode Island. But my eyes, much bigger than my talent, were focused on a host of better jobs and brighter lights outside of New England.

My hopes were high as I answered eight help-wanted ads for anchors in an industry publication, sending each prospect a résumé and a tape of my latest show. But my hopes diminished as, one after another, my submissions were returned, rejected. Frustrated, I tore open each package and popped the tapes into the video player, trying to figure out what had gone wrong. Three of my returned tapes showed that each news director had watched only ten seconds before stopping the tape. Each had known in just ten seconds they did not want me! Were they looking for a man, I wondered. Maybe an African-American or Asian woman. Or was I just that bad?

Spirits low, I slunk over to the anchor desk and tried to find something to be confident about. After the newscast, the telephone rang and a wild and crazy guy was on the line—a celebrated hair stylist with a reputation for speaking his mind.

"Darling, Darling, you are so wonderful doing the news . . . but your hair, Darling, it looks like a piece of s—t. You come to me, Darling, I will make you beautiful."

Instead of being offended, I grabbed on to the life preserver he was throwing my way.

The mousy brunette who walked in his salon slunk out a Marilyn Monroe blonde. The change stunned me so much that I wanted to find a bag to cover my head. Though I begged the stylist to put me back the way I was, he would not be altered from his course.

"Try it, Darling, you'll like it," he cooed. I left crying.

The next night I taped my show and watched it. The sparkling, blond hair definitely added luster to this novice anchor's appearance. I watched the tape intently and became inspired. My motivational juices kicked in. I made duplicate copies of my new look and sent them along with my old résumé to the same eight news directors who had just sent me form-letter rejections.

This time, six of the eight wanted to see more of my work. I sent it out, landed one of those anchor jobs, and have remained a blonde ever since. These days, however, I'm a blonde not to please them; I'm a blonde to please me.

## BE WILLING TO CHANGE

Self-motivation and change are inseparable. Successful women don't fear change, they embrace it. They are open and receptive to new ideas, and you should be, too. Start adding new dimensions to your life. Look forward to new experiences and try approaching them in a new and different way.

You can't rewrite the past. From this moment on, however, you can shape your future—but only if you look forward to change with anticipation rather than fear.

I know it's uncomfortable to give up the old, familiar choices, even if they're poor choices. That's why many women stay with their abusive spouses. Often, it's easier to suffer with the devil they know than to take a chance on the devil they don't know. But as my mom says, "If things don't change, they'll remain the same." She is a master of understatement.

Think of it this way: it's not really out with the old and in with the new. It's more a matter of altering the "old you" into a wonderful "new you." You accomplish that by changing your attitudes and habits.

# CHECK OUT YOUR ATTITUDE

Attitudes, as we discuss in Chapter 3, are the way we act, think, and feel. An action, a thought, or a feeling becomes a habit through repetition. Our attitudes and habits were formed early in life. They're ingrained. The experts say at least ninety-five percent of what we do each day is done from habit. We react instinctively to every situation that arises on any given day. Without even realizing it, we have formed habits to cover almost everything we do, such as getting behind the wheel of the car. We don't think, "Okay, I have to release the parking brake. I need to put the key in. I need to turn the key." We just do it. It's automatic. It's habit.

Habits are difficult to change. After all, we've been following a particular set of rules for a long time. My mother, for example, always thought brown was my color. It never was. It was her color and she dressed me in it for years. When I moved out on my own, I kept buying brown suits, brown skirts, and brown shoes. One day I tried on a wonderful black and bright red outfit and became transformed. The little mouse blossomed, and I felt bright, successful, and—yes—even powerful. I adjusted my attitude, changed my habits, and never bought brown clothes again. And I never will.

Falling back on old familiar habits and attitudes is often the path of least resistance. Even though many of these are unhealthy for us, we still find comfort drawing from the same old well. Walking away from the devil we know is a challenge, but it's worth the effort. Don't be bound by the precedents of yesterday. Motivate yourself for change, but be very careful about the method you choose. There are many different ways to motivate yourself. Not all of them are healthy.

## FEAR MAKES YOU MOVE

No doubt about it. Fear makes us move, but the question is, "Will we be headed in the right direction?"

Fear is a great motivator, but it's also dangerous and destructive. Business and industry use fear motivation all the time. Downsizing, bean-counting, pay cuts, layoffs, demotions, and dismissal—words that can make our hearts race, our heads pound, and our mouths turn dry.

A news director who used fear motivation nearly destroyed me. At first my work level soared, and for a brief time I reached new heights, bringing in one exclusive after another. But in the end, I allowed him to wear me down, becoming nothing more than a workhorse. I lost my individuality and my stamina. My work became second-rate. Instead of putting all my energy into my job, I allowed it to be drained by the effort it took to tolerate the high level of stress he was handing out. I spent more time being afraid of him than doing my job.

Instead of becoming a leader in the newsroom, I became an insecure, fear-ridden follower. Sacrificing my determination for defensiveness, I became very inefficient. Instead of digging up stories, I spent my days dealing with fear and trying to avoid the news director's wrath. I could no longer be my best and do my best.

We can never be leaders if we don't recognize fear for what it is and rid ourselves of it. A steady diet of fear ultimately chokes our best efforts to find success.

A woman locked in an abusive relationship accepts fear as a natural part of life. She is plagued by two devils, one on the outside, the other within.

Verbal abuse is often her constant companion, dished out by the man who was supposed to honor and respect her "as long as we both shall live."

She might be a leader in her community, but when she goes home she steps into a world filled with shadows. In the eyes of her husband, she can't do anything right. She spends her days walking on eggshells and her nights tip-toeing around controversy. Anything can set him off, and anything does. So she bends over backward not to aggravate him, but he always finds something about which to get angry.

It's difficult to explain to someone who has not experienced fear motivation how one could stay in such a world and put up with all the danger and distress on a daily basis. "Just walk away," they say. What they don't understand is that when someone is constantly motivated by fear, she develops a tolerance for it. Fear becomes an acceptable part of life.

And it's not just the devil on the outside doing all the damage. The effort it takes to maintain the status quo in such a negative atmosphere creates one big ball of stress inside. As it grows and shifts, it tears the woman apart. First, her spirit breaks down, then her health. Her personality changes and she starts making poor value judgments. Fear motivation corrodes her well-being just as rust covers the lawn furniture left out last winter. Ultimately, there is no joy, no peace, and no comfort.

If this describes you, what you have to remember in a situation like this is that personal leadership rests on strength of character, not on marching to the beat of a bad drummer. You can turn your situation around. Don't wait for someone to offer to help, or for the abuse to escalate until you become severely injured. You can motivate yourself out of trouble.

That's exactly what Mary Anne did. I met her in 1990 at a motivational seminar I was presenting on how to stop fearing life and start living it. She was drawn to my message like iron to a magnet, and after the seminar ended she asked for a private moment with me to talk about her life.

Mary Anne, it seems, had gone through a life of hell with her abusive spouse. One day, when she had finally had enough, she decided to remove herself safely from the situation. She became determined to cease being motivated by fear. She said it was as simple as that.

"Something snapped inside of me one day," she told me, "and I decided I no longer had to live in fear. I was tired and angry. Every decision I had made in our married life revolved around not upsetting him. It was time to start thinking about me. I called in a lawyer and together we worked out a plan to get me safely out of the house. I began to map out my future that day and never looked back. I will never be motivated by fear again."

Whenever we allow fear to motivate us, there always seems to be an unpleasant payoff. There are much better and healthier ways to motivate yourself. Don't deal in fear.

## WHAT'S IN IT FOR ME?

Another type of motivation that moves many of us is one that promises rewards. Are you still searching for your own personal pot of gold at the end of the rainbow? Do you often ask yourself, "What's in it for me?" before tackling the task at hand? If so, you're employing what's called reward or incentive motivation.

Basically, this comes from a barter system that gets started early in life. When you were a little girl, remember how your parents or grandparents offered you candy or ice cream in exchange for promises of good behavior?

You've matured through the years and so have your desires. Your needs and wants have become more sophisticated. In addition to the basics—food, shelter, clothing, and safety—you also seek recognition, praise, and prestige. You motivate yourself *just enough* to get those things. And this is where the problem comes in.

This kind of motivation is not sustaining. It ends when you get what you want. Reward motivation does not build character. It lacks permanence because it has no lasting effect on your personality. It does not encourage any positive behavior modification. While it's probably not as harmful as fear motivation, reward motivation can damage your value system. Using this method of motivation could encourage you to become more materialistic and less focused on what's really important in life.

## ON YOUR MARK, GET SET. . . .

I've thrived for years on competition motivation. Pitting myself against another person to win the prize really gets my juices flowing. Sadly, the desire to improve myself is not enough; I seem to need the thrill of the hunt. Here's a case in point.

I love the game of golf. Even though I have a strong desire to consistently score in the low 80s (which for you non-golfers is a great score for a recreational golfer), I seem to lack the necessary motivation to do what needs to be done: to get out there on the driving range and practice, practice, practice.

Understanding my own personality, I figured my golf game wouldn't improve unless I challenged myself in some way. So I joined a women's league. Every Tuesday morning, I put my new-found talent to the test. Although I've won on many occasions, it's the losing that spurs me into action. After every loss, my competition motivation kicks in, and you'll find me out on the driving range doing what I hate the most, practicing.

It's what I should have been doing all along if I had been properly motivated. As a result, my game has improved. When you consider that only 20 percent of today's golfers consistently score below 100, my average score in the high 80s–low 90s puts me on top of more than 80 percent of the men and women.

Being competitive means pulling out all the stops and putting our talents to the test. We become motivated when we set our sights on a goal and take the necessary steps to get results. We work hard and become educated about what it will take to win the pot of gold at the end of the rainbow. But we have to apply caution to this method of motivation. It has a major drawback.

When we compete we continually compare ourselves to others. On the up side, the comparison makes us feel better and stronger about ourselves.

But on the flip side, comparison with others as a way of identifying oneself can devastate or demoralize an already damaged self-image.

Plus, this kind of motivation is not sustaining. Once you take home the trophy, where do you go from there? Like "Short-Time Susie," you've shot your wad and lost the desire to stay motivated. As far as you're concerned, it's done, finished, over.

# DO THE RIGHT THING . . .
# IT'S THE ONLY WAY TO GO

Start today to motivate yourself by results rather than methods. Stop relying on the promise of a reward or the fear of punishment to force you to move forward. Do it because it's the right thing to do.

There is only one type of motivation that has staying power and makes an impact on your life in a positive, long-term manner. It's a planned program of self-motivation based on the development of good basic attitudes and habits.

Expect to see some results of self-motivation immediately. Other results will be harder to spot because often they're longer range and intangible. But remember, even when you can't see the obvious benefit, you're still moving forward to the realization of your dreams and desires.

# CHAPTER 6

# STEP FOUR:
# CLEAR ALL OBSTACLES FROM YOUR PATH

*"The way I see it, if you want the rainbow,*
*you gotta put up with the rain."*

—*Dolly Parton*

Spending a day with Oprah Winfrey is like getting your diploma from the School of Hard Knocks without ever feeling the pain. Oprah is a walking textbook on how to overcome all obstacles to find success. Her rise from an abusive childhood to the Fortune 500 list is legendary among the millions of women who look to her as a role model. She's an African-American Cinderella, but instead of having a fairy godmother, she's blessed with a strong work ethic and great instincts.

"Follow your instincts," Oprah told me. "That's where true wisdom manifests itself."

I've interviewed Oprah on four separate occasions, and each time I've walked away knowing a little more about her but much more about me. Successful women have a way of doing that. They make you think about yourself while you're finding out about them. They inspire you without trying to do so. As you listen to their particular story of success, you become motivated to do more with your own life. Oprah triumphed over a young life filled with pain, misery, and mistakes to become a woman of achievement. Anyone can do the same. All you have to do is take her advice, which she dispenses readily.

During my most recent chat with Oprah, we greeted each other in her Chicago television studio long after the audience had gone. She had taped two shows that day and was starting to wear out. She led me to the back corner of the set to a cozy area in the style of a living room. We sat down together on the sofa. As my camera rolled, she answered all my questions with the blunt honesty and the humor for which she's noted.

Then things got serious. I asked Oprah how she had managed to turn her life around—a life marred by sexual abuse, drugs, teen pregnancy, and rock-bottom self-esteem. Oprah looked me squarely in the eye, leaned in closely, and said, "Donna, you've got to clear your path. Girl, you've got to clear your path."

## SIX FRIENDS OF FAILURE

Six deadly demotivators stand between you and your success: worry, doubt, negativity, guilt, jealousy, and the one we touched on briefly in the last chapter, fear. Nothing good or positive ever flows into a life filled with these six friends of failure. The bad triumphs by quickly choking off the good.

When everything starts going right in your life, do you suddenly find yourself feeling negative, fearful, doubtful, or guilty?

Do you worry you won't be able to maintain your success? Or are you jealous because even with all your hard work, someone else seems to be getting more than you? How much time do you waste looking over your shoulder, waiting for one or more of the evil six to creep up on you? As Oprah would say, it's time to clear your path to move ahead.

Expecting these six meddlesome enemies of success to interfere with your life has become a conditioned response learned from years of overuse—in other words, a bad habit. It's time to toughen up and start exorcizing these six demons that keep you at arm's length from a better, more pleasurable life.

No one else can rescue you from a life haunted by fear, worry, doubt, negativity, guilt, and jealousy. You have to do that yourself. Start by closely examining some of the dangerous demotivators in your life.

## WHICH ONES PLAGUE YOU?

Take a look at the worksheet on the next page. I invite you to spend some time listing the obstacles to your personal success.

List the things that cause you worry. What do you fear? What kinds of doubts do you have about yourself? What makes you feel guilty and jealous?

Finally, list some of the negative attitudes that have kept you from achieving.

# WHAT'S HOLDING YOU BACK?

## DANGEROUS DEMOTIVATORS

**FEAR:**

**WORRY:**

**DOUBT:**

**NEGATIVITY:**

**GUILT:**

**JEALOUSY:**

It sounds like a frightening thing to do, putting so many negative things down on paper in black and white, but the exercise is actually cleansing. Once you write them down, you've identified them. They are no longer vague apprehensions swirling around in your subconscious. Once you identify them, you can begin to tackle them one by one, as I did with my own fears.

I used to worry every Sunday morning when I opened the newspaper. You see, there's a feature called the "TV Hotline" in our Sunday paper. Viewers write in and express their likes and dislikes about local television. Most of the letters published about me through the years have been positive, but what I feared every Sunday was opening up the paper and spotting an ugly letter. No matter how many good ones had been printed, I fearfully searched for the bad one. I conditioned myself to look for it every week, even though on only three Sundays in *ten years* had my fears been realized. And on those three occasions, I had become satisfied, almost happy, that my worst fear had been realized. Even though it conveyed bad news, something I had worried about actually came true.

I performed the same ritual every Sunday morning. Aroused from my slumber, I got out of bed, slipped on my husband's oversized raincoat and shoes, tiptoed out through the garage, and scooped up the paper. Then I carried it into the kitchen and put it on the counter. The coffee perked while I spread it out, gave a cursory check to the day's news, and then slowly, inexorably moved toward the entertainment section, almost savoring the dread as I inhaled the aroma of the brewing coffee.

Every Sunday I feared the worst, and one Sunday I was not disappointed. The bold, black headline screamed, "Enough of Jordan." The letter accused me of one flagrant breach of good taste after another. Of course, all the accusations were untrue, making me believe this was a mean-spirited attack by a master of misstatement. To make matters worse, I felt exposed for all the world to see, while the anonymity of the poison pen wielder was protected. This was a vicious attack, and there wasn't a thing I could do about it, except worry what effect it might have on my career and my life. "What will everybody think when they see that letter? Will they believe that bilge? How will my boss react?"

In retrospect, I understand why I feared the "bad" letter so much. It was because it *reaffirmed my own fears about not being good enough.*

What about you?

It took me years as a television anchor to learn you can't please everyone, no matter how hard you try. And you can't get upset because a person who doesn't even know you goes on a very personal attack. There are some extremely small people out there who relish knocking other people down so they can feel better about themselves—people who seriously need to get a life. Lacking one of their own, they affect yours by whipping out their poison pens, and, in my case, by spewing their venom in the newspaper for all the world to see. But remember, these nasty actions negatively affect your life only if you let them. You have the power to rise above this kind of attack.

The same thing happens to Oprah all the time. For the first few years of her celebrity, she was the media's darling and had nothing to fear from the press. And then the spiteful and untrue articles began appearing in the daily rags. She became hurt and fearful. Oprah told me the last straw was when her best friends started believing what they read and began questioning her about it.

That was the day, Oprah told me, she decided she would stop being fearful. "I realized, Donna, that these people don't even know me. The people who say these cruel things and make up these stories don't even know anything about me. So why should I give them the power to upset me?"

After years of feeling similarly fearful, I took a cue from Oprah. I pledged to stop feeling as if I'd given up the ghost by allowing these mean-spirited letters to haunt me. I came to realize that nothing I could ever do would please these curmudgeons. Unhappy with life, they hate your success. They spend their days searching for mistakes and miscues because that's what it takes for them to feel important in life. They're not going to change, but I can—by being positive, not worrying, and looking fear right in the eye without blinking.

# DEMOTIVATOR 1: FEAR

Fear is the feeling of dread or anxiety we experience when danger is near, or the vague apprehension that overwhelms us when real pain is imminent. Fear can overtake us any time, in any place. It can either galvanize us into action or freeze us into immobility. It's all in the way we handle it.

On the plus side, fear is a necessary part of self-preservation that can save a life. It alerts the body in an emergency, as a smoke detector warns of imminent danger. When we're physically or psychologically threatened, the fear alarm goes off, sending the mind and body into action to protect ourselves. That is fear at its best.

What becomes problematic, however, is when we react to the perception of the situation rather than the reality of it. We *think* a threat is imminent, so our brains put our bodies on alert even though there's no real danger or pain. That is when fear changes from a lifesaver into a demotivator.

If our needs are not being satisfied, or we think there's even a chance they won't be, our fear mechanism can sometimes kick in inappropriately. We become consumed with saving ourselves from a situation that doesn't require rescue. We lose sight of our goals and what's really important in life. Fear stifles our creativity and smothers our decision-making process. We begin to feel overwhelmed, frustrated, and hopeless, wasting time and energy by totally overreacting to the situation. We feel pressured, and good ideas are lost as fear stirs us up inside and creates stress.

It happened to me while writing this very chapter. One morning, I sat down at the computer at 5:00 A.M. I wanted to complete half a chapter before going in to work at the television station. I was really rolling that morning. The words were flowing from my fingertips as I sat and banged out Chapter 6. I felt inspired. I felt as if every word I typed was golden. I had reached deep inside myself and pulled out some very strong messages on how fear can shortcut success. As I scrolled back the screen and reread what I had written, I felt very self-satisfied. This would be my best chapter yet. Then, outside my library window, I heard a skid and a crash as a car slammed into a power pole. The lights inside my home flickered and surged, and the computer took a hit. I watched, horrified, as the screen turned into black nothingness. My message was gone. I had neglected to punch the save key. All was lost.

I sat there stunned, staring at the dead monitor. Beyond disappointment and rage, I felt fear. Fear that I would never be able to recapture my first fleeting thoughts, which I believed were so profound. Fear that I wouldn't be successful. Fear that I would fail. Fear that momentarily blocked out my concern about the safety of the driver, who, as it turned out, was shaken up but not injured.

When fear moved in, my common sense moved out. I became crippled as fear blocked my creativity. I couldn't calm down enough to quickly rewrite the message while it was still in my memory. Fear blocked my concentration. Instead of working through my problem, I focused only on the evil thing that had happened, and going through a litany of, "Oh, why didn't I stop when I first wanted to and my work would have been saved! Why did I have to write that one last paragraph?" Two thousand wonderful words gone in the blink of an electric light.

Fear immobilized me for about a half hour. Then I calmed down and thought the situation over carefully. What's two thousand words in the big picture of life? I still have my talent, my ability, and my drive to finish. I summoned up my courage and met my fear head-on. I sat back down and started again. Some of my original ideas are lost forever, but others, even better than before, appeared magically on the screen—once my fear dissipated and my frozen fingers thawed out.

As you may have discovered in dealing with one of your own crises, fear becomes a deadly demotivator when it becomes your usual way of doing business, even when there's no threat to you and your environment. When fear becomes your standard operating procedure, you trade in your future for your present. You cannot look forward if you need to spend all your time overcoming daily fears and sidestepping the kind of confrontation that helps you grow. You find it much easier to say "I'm frightened" than to face your fear. Apprehension and dread become a daily part of your life. Soon, there will be no joy, no peace, and no room for achievement.

Living with fear as a constant companion saps our strength, kills our potential for growth, and puts stress on our bodies. We become exhausted as the adrenaline pumps and our muscles tense to keep our bodies in full fear-alert status. We tire mentally, as well, from the amount of concentration needed to overcome a particular fear and take action. What a waste. Think about it. We could be using all those physical and psychological factors to our advantage, but instead we're just scattering our forces to the wind.

Take a look at your list of fears on your worksheet. How many are based on perception rather than reality? Do they really pose a serious threat to your safety and health? I'd be surprised if they do.

Another strength-sapper is basing your fears on what *other people think, say, or do.* Do you waste time being frightened about what others are saying about you? Why is what everybody else thinks more important than what you want? These are fears based on an active imagination rather than on any real threat. Even though such fears have no basis in fact, you still become frightened, distrustful, anxious, or even panicked by them.

These fears are artificially created and destructive. They erode our self-image and undermine our self-confidence.

There are only two acceptable ways to handle fear. One is by applying caution and beating a hasty retreat, safely removing ourselves from the situation. This method is often best in matters of personal safety. If we're being threatened by a group of dangerous thugs, handing over what they want and backing out of danger is probably the best way of handling it. Confrontation in a hostile environment could result in severe injury.

The second way of handling fear is to be courageous and meet our challenges head on. I believe the only true way we can conquer a fear is by facing it down, and in most cases I prefer using courage over caution.

Courage is the best weapon we have to fight fear. There is much to be won by showing people our true mettle. Handle your own fears firmly. Control them instead of allowing them to control you.

Expect to feel overwhelmed the first time you try to summon up your courage to fight fear. After all, you've spent years conditioning yourself to believe you can't do it, and then, when you finally can, you're amazed at what you've accomplished. As Franklin D. Roosevelt said, "The only thing we have to fear is fear itself." Fear can handcuff you, thereby keeping success out of your reach. Only courage provides the key to unlock those cuffs.

Once we recognize fear for what it really is—an ineffective habit—we want to change. And the only way to do that is with courage.

## DEMOTIVATOR 2: WORRY

How many years have you spent worrying about things over which you have absolutely no control? How many hours have you spent fretting about something bad that never happened? How many people have you annoyed with your disquieting state of uneasiness? How much valuable time are you wasting with your vague apprehensions and concerns over things you can't change?

Worry is a troubled state of mind, a prolonged, exaggerated fear, basically borrowing trouble before it's due. It often strikes us when we're facing a new experience in life and are unable to influence it or to predict the outcome—like knowing your seventy-year-old parents are about to hop in their car and drive halfway across the country to come visit you.

You worry about their safety and all the terrible things that could befall them. But they've made up their minds, and driving is what they want to do. There is nothing you can do to influence their decision or to affect the outcome of their journey. So you worry. Worry that the car might not stay in one piece. Worry that they'll be in an accident. Worry that they'll drive too long and tire themselves. Worry that the stress of the long drive could tax their hearts. Worry that as senior citizens they may cut financial corners and stay at an unsafe motel. Worry that they'll miss their meals and Dad will forget his insulin shot.

By the time they arrive at your home, you are a nervous wreck. They've had a great time traveling across the country. What a wonderful, exciting adventure they've had. They feel stimulated, alive, and delighted to see their wonderful daughter. But as they walk into your house, you begin to scold them like children because they worried you.

You punish *them* for the distress *you* felt while they were having the time of their lives reasserting their independence. Your worry makes their visit start off on the wrong foot.

Decide today to stop borrowing trouble before it's due. Our paths to success are already strewn with enough obstacles. We don't need to add one more to swerve around. We can become better and stronger immediately by assessing our worries and determining whether we have the power to make each one disappear.

Whenever worry starts negatively affecting your life, grab a sheet of paper and list everything troubling you. Don't leave out anything. Examine the list closely. Assess each item by asking the same question: "What constructive action can I take to remove this worry from my mind?" The answer to that question becomes your plan of action. In other words, determine that you *do* have control over this particular worry and that it's time to exert it.

But what happens if we run up against a worry over which we have no influence or control? What I do is to turn the worry over to a higher power. In my case, I pray to God and ask God to lift the burden from my shoulders. I have always found strength in that release and believe that the issue about which I'm worried couldn't be placed in better hands.

We have to let go of the worries we can't change. It's essential for our well-being and future success. Rather than sitting and stewing about things that are out of our control, we are better served by focusing our mental energies on the issues and problems we can do something about. Take care of what we can and let go of what we can't.

# DEMOTIVATOR 3: DOUBT

You're playing tennis. It's your turn to serve. You step up to the line, bounce the ball once, and then hesitate. There's a lot at stake. Your opponents are one point away from winning the tournament. This serve is for all the marbles. You become frightened and doubtful. You have to be careful not to give the point away; make them work for it if they're going to win. Don't just hand the victory over like a big, fat turkey on the Thanksgiving Day platter. There's no honor in that.

Your partner is pinning all her hopes on you. The worst thing that could happen now would be for you to double fault, to not get either serve in the box. That would be an automatic win for the opposing team and make you look stupid, like a weak person who can't handle a little pressure.

You begin to falter. You look at the watching crowd and wonder what they'll think of you if you double fault. Instead of concentrating on serving up a winner, you become

consumed with the prospect of failure. All your concentration now rests on not double faulting rather than on what
it takes to successfully get the job done. You start chanting
to yourself, "I can't double fault, I can't double fault."

Self-doubt begins to smother you, eroding your mental
toughness. Instead of visualizing the perfect serve and concentrating on it hitting powerfully into the box, you let your
lack of conviction overtake you. You focus on the negative.
Double faulting is all you can think about. You begin to
believe that a double fault now is not only possible but prob-
able.

You toss the ball up in the air for the first serve, swing,
and miss the box by a mile. You bounce the second ball as
the remainder of your conviction drifts away. You falter,
bounce the ball again, toss it high in the air, and the inevi-
table happens. You double fault. After all, what did you
really expect? All that self-doubt manifested itself in the
thing you feared the most.

Doubt is basically an internalized fear. In the case of the
double fault, it's the conviction we lack when we don't trust
ourselves. As soon as we begin to doubt our ability, we lose
confidence in the strong serve that ordinarily is an important part of our arsenal, and we lose the courage to fall back
on years of experience and training. Doubt also robs us of
the mental toughness it takes to become a champion.

Doubt can negatively affect every opportunity for success in our lives if we let it. No matter what our present
state, our future is abundant with new challenges destined
to sail us into uncharted waters where our character and
strength will be tested repeatedly. If we fear the unknown
and allow nagging self-doubts to keep us from accepting
and embracing these challenges, we never grow into the
person we have the potential to become.

Don't let doubt rob your future.

Others of us doubt because we fear making mistakes. It's often easier to go with the flow and to not put our talents to the test, because we don't want to fail. Or perhaps we tried something once and failed, so we refuse to challenge ourselves again. Well, we all make mistakes. There's no woman on earth who doesn't. We cannot keep avoiding failure and mistakes for the rest of our lives. The way we handle mistakes is what separates the winners from the losers.

Learn from your mistakes, and you gain strength.

We also invite doubt into our lives when we fear things we don't know or don't understand. What happens when somebody shows you a new way of doing something? Does "that will never work" become your first reaction? How about when you meet people of another race, another culture? Do you concentrate on the differences instead of the similarities and doubt you could ever have a relationship, so you don't even try? If so, you're missing out on some wonderful opportunities to broaden your world and experience new and different things in your life. Doubt distances us from obtaining what we most want out of life.

There are only two ways to handle doubt. The first is the worst. Unfortunately, it's the chosen method for too many women. Content to sit on the sidelines of life, these "doubting Thomasinas" make doubt habitual. It's their common response to everything. As soon as a new situation arises, they feel doubt. As soon as life gets a bit sticky, they feel doubt. Not wanting to make a mistake, they feel doubt. Being too lazy to gather the facts necessary to make informed decisions, they feel doubt. Calling doubt forth in almost every situation is one of the quickest ways to cut off success.

The second way is to find courage and become a confident decision-maker. Gather all the facts you can. The more information you possess, the better armed you will be to make informed decisions. If you were going into battle, you'd arm yourself with the best weapons you could find, right? Well, it's the same thing when you make decisions or choices—arm yourself with every scrap of information you can dig out. Then there will be no room for doubt.

That's what I do when writing a television news story. Turning over rocks and looking for obscure pieces of information is now part of my daily routine. I've become comfortable with this method, but it wasn't always like that. I used to experience doubt, worry, and fear every time the boss handed me an assignment. I feared making a mistake, worried about not being able to gather the correct information, and doubted I had enough talent to put it all together and write a solid story. However, these fears dissipated once I summoned my courage and began to move forward toward the realization of my goal—in this case, the successful completion of my news story.

The very act of taking action eases fear and quells doubt. My confidence level rose as I began gathering all the facts and evaluating them. Things began to fall into place as I moved forward with confidence. The more information I got, the more easily I wrote the story. After each story was completed and turned in, I sat back and wondered why I had wasted so much time doubting myself. The job was complete, I didn't miss my deadline, and the story was good. Why did I put myself through all that added stress?

Fear, worry, and doubt can control you only if you lack self-confidence. Build your self-confidence and these three enemies of success will disappear. *Substitute courage for fear, motivation for worry, and confidence for doubt.*

# DEMOTIVATOR 4: NEGATIVITY

Being negative is a bad habit that's hard to break. And a habit is exactly what negativity is. It often starts early in childhood. Many of us acquire this crippling demotivator from our parents. Parents who were conditioned to respond negatively to life pass their limiting attitudes on to their children, who may have entirely different talents and abilities. Parents don't mean to do this—it just happens.

When I was a child, I dreamed of growing up to become Miss America. To do that, I would need a talent. After an honest appraisal of my singing voice, I decided dancing would be just the ticket. I begged my mother for dancing lessons, but she was opposed. She could see no benefits from my squeezing into toe or tap shoes. All she could envision was the risk of failure.

"I hate seeing girls with no ability clumping around like horses on the stage," she said. "Everyone giggles and laughs at their mistakes. They get embarrassed and hurt."

What she was really saying is *she* always preferred sacrificing possible achievement to the risk of embarrassment. Her statement echoed *her* low self-esteem and lack of self-confidence. Because she loved me, she wanted to spare me from what, to her, represented failure, but I heard something quite different. I believed she had no confidence in me and would be embarrassed by my mistakes. I also believed that if Mom thought I would not be successful, I probably wouldn't be, so why try? Unfortunately, this was not the last time I walked away from a challenge because of a negative attitude.

Negative conditioning permeated our young lives. "*Don't* leave the table until you've finished everything on your plate. *Don't* chew with your mouth full. *Don't* run out in the street. *Don't* jump off that stone wall. *Don't* touch that hot stove." These are all negative phrases our parents used in hopes of achieving a positive result—to keep us out of harm's way.

Our parents didn't realize what they were doing to us. In addition to achieving their objective, their daily dose of negativity made us fearful and stifled our creativity. The litany of don'ts that Mom and Dad recited on a daily basis sent us very strong negative messages. And as we grew older, another player, society, entered the game of negative conditioning.

Today, society bombards us with all sorts of negative messages, until I begin to wonder if there's anybody left on the planet who first looks for the bright side of things. These messages have great impact. One look at the nightly newscast will show you what I mean.

Here you find one shocking and gruesome story after another. If it isn't about murder and sex, it's a frightening story about what Uncle Sam will or won't do for you. Newscasts are filled with shocking stories that people absorb and talk about around the office water cooler the next day. Whenever these people are polled, they say they want more positive news on the air. Yet television news ratings indicate differently.

What gets you to stop punching the channel changer long enough to let it cool down? I'd be willing to bet it's the sensational story that grabs your interest and holds your attention for more than a moment. I once worked for a television station that believed in giving people the good news they said they wanted. The station began showing as much good news as possible and lots of soft feature stories. People tuned out in record numbers. People say they prefer positive news to negative, but you couldn't prove it by that station's experience.

Look at what happened to Oprah Winfrey when she decided to fight back against negativity. She decided to take a firm stand against the overwhelming tide of sleaze and sensationalism in today's talk shows, opting for the high road with shows that educate rather than titillate. The critics applauded her mightily, but some of her audience tuned out. You will no longer see outrageous behavior or salacious topics on Oprah's show, but she paid the price when her ratings took a dip. People tune in to see the dirt. She wasn't offering it, so some of her viewers went elsewhere. Still, Oprah refused to be swayed from her principles, and has held steadfastly to her values. As a result, she has won over a growing legion of fans who, like their hero, accent the positive.

Negativity is a poison. It takes root in the brain and quickly pulses throughout the entire body and well-being. It infects everything it touches. One of the first symptoms of this disease, which handicaps our minds as well as our futures, is a change in attitude. Instead of looking on the bright side, its victims search for the dark clouds and openly state their opinions and beliefs for anyone who will listen. Negative people are usually chronic complainers. They are always unhappy.

There are four types of complainers in the world. The first is the *whiner*. This woman can never be satisfied with anything. She constantly looks at what she doesn't have rather than at what she does. She feels life has dealt her an unfair hand. When the chips are down, this woman will do anything to protect herself, even at the expense of others. She is selfish, envious, and tiresome. She's "cried wolf" so many times that no one takes her seriously. Whiners have no credibility; they therefore receive no respect and earn no admiration.

Then there's the *martyr.* This woman always feels picked on. "Poor little me," is her battle cry. "What could I have possibly done to make you put this burden on me?" This woman is so miserable she makes others feel miserable, too. She spreads negativity wherever she goes. No matter how much attention you show this woman, it's never enough. She always believes nobody appreciates her. And after operating like this for a while, she is correct.

The *cynic* operates on a different level. This is the woman who thinks everybody and everything is wrong. Nothing has meaning for the cynic. Nothing is new enough, big enough, or bright enough. If she were to win a prize, she would hesitate to accept it, because if the prize were good enough for her to win, how good could it be? It can't be much of a prize.

The fourth type of complainer is the *perfectionist.* No matter how hard any of us tries, we can never measure up to this woman's expectations. You do your best to try to please her, but her look of disdain says, "Is that really the best you can do?" Perfectionists rob you of your joy in life if you let them. The perfectionist creates unrealistic goals for herself and for others. She always looks at what's not completed instead of what is. Never satisfied, she fails to find comfort or pleasure in life. She constantly questions life instead of enjoying it. Perfectionism can destroy friendships, damage marriages, and cost careers. It can break your spirit.

Complaining destroys joy. It makes us and the people around us miserable. What good does it do to complain? Does it get the job done? No. In fact, often it stands in the way of the successful completion of our tasks. But there is good news. With a little work, anyone can overcome this negative conditioning.

As Gloria Steinem says, "The first problem for all of us . . . is not to learn, but to unlearn." A personality shaped by daily exposure to negativism can be changed by daily exposure to more positive influences. Shape your own destiny and don't let outside forces propel you toward the negative. The very absence of complaining and arguing will make you a standout in life.

First, look for the good in every situation. Don't be so habituated to grab hold of the bad just because it's quick and easy. Start by being grateful for what you have—not just the material gifts, but your unique talents and abilities, too. Develop an attitude of gratitude and don't take any positive thing for granted. Often, people who have the most find little or no value in it. They become jaded in their search for bigger and better. Don't let that happen to you. Stop to appreciate what you have instead of always looking at what you don't have. Put a positive spin on any situation that confronts you.

Next, really listen to what's coming out of your mouth. Speak to build up, not to tear down. The old adage, "If you can't say something nice about someone, don't say anything," is true. Don't let your words be hurtful or harmful. Try to make all your criticism of others the constructive kind, and don't fall victim to gossip. Gossiping erodes your well-being. It is negative by its very nature. Be more concerned with building others up than with knocking them down.

Also, speak well about yourself. Always build yourself up. Never tear yourself down. You do that by monitoring your self-talk. Really start listening to what you are saying. If your vocabulary is filled with a lot of "I can'ts" and "I don't think I cans," get rid of them. Find a better and more positive way of communicating.

Take a few moments and look at the worksheet on the opposite page. List all the negative things you usually say about yourself and others—things such as, "I'll never be able to do the job."

Each time you hear yourself utter a negative phrase, jot it down.

After you've written down all the negative examples of self-talk in your life, work to find a more positive spin for each statement. Write that positive statement in the next column. For example, "I'll never be able to do the job," now changes to, "It's going to be a challenge, but I can get the job done."

As I mentioned earlier, when you write something down, you focus attention on it. Once you put a spotlight on a problem, you can make it fade away. Every time you utter a negative phrase, write it down and then find a better way—a more positive way—of saying it. You won't have to do this long.

Pretty soon, you will start self-correcting in your mind, and you'll stop speaking negatively—about yourself and others.

Through the years, I've learned another valuable tool to fight negativity: Don't let poor self-confidence or a negative self-image make you share your weak points with another human being, especially one in power. If these weak points do indeed exist, they will stand out all by themselves. They don't need you as a flag person pointing them out. Instead, operate from a position of strength. Reveal only good things about yourself to another person. Associate yourself with the strong and the positive right from the start, and others will see you the same way. Remember, perception is reality.

# START TALKING SMART

## SOUNDS LIKE THE *OLD* YOU:

## SOUNDS LIKE THE *NEW* YOU:

How many times has this happened to you? You are sitting in the boss's office and the talk turns to your particular talents and abilities. Even though you want to show your stuff and be at your best, somehow you feel obligated to list your shortcomings and try to explain them away. After this litany, you start listing all the positives. By that time, it's too late. You have already done the damage and encouraged your employer to look at you with a jaundiced eye. Without realizing it, you lose twice. First, you lose the boss's respect, and then you lose respect for yourself. You walk away from the office feeling small and insignificant, once again focusing all your attention on the negative.

One day I sat in my boss's office. She was new to the job, hired just after I was. She noted that she'd never seen me anchor a broadcast and was excited to see what I could do. My first impulse was to be super-critical and explain away some of my weaker points, which she would be sure to notice. That's when something snapped inside me, like the rubber band on a smoker's wrist warning her not to take that next puff. So I broke my negative habit, quickly shrugging off the impulse and adopting a positive style. I began to list my strong points to explain what I could do to help her enhance the anchor team. She was pleased and reassured. My strong self-image propelled me from an underling to a colleague. Recognizing my value, she sees me on a peer level and respects both my advice and my opinions.

One other note: start looking at the big picture instead of all the petty annoyances that plague you daily. Accept the fact that life isn't fair. It never has been. It never will be. You have to do what's right and positive for you while trying to not hurt another person. All the whining in the world will not level the playing field. Neither will being a martyr, a cynic, or a perfectionist.

# DEMOTIVATOR 5: GUILT

Have you ever told a half-truth or a lie that ended up hurting someone? How did you feel—guilty? You should have. By its very definition, guilt is the state of having done wrong or committed an offense.

We do the damage, then we feel guilty about it. That's how our guilt mechanism is supposed to work. The problem arises when guilt is used at the wrong time. When our guilt reflex kicks in for no good reason, it turns an effective mechanism for determining right from wrong into a deadly demotivator. And when it happens repeatedly, it becomes a destructive habit.

Like other demotivators, guilt is something that takes root in childhood. It's a feeling of self-reproach that comes from believing we have done wrong. The operative word in that sentence is "believing." More often than not, we have absolutely nothing to feel reproachful or guilty about, but some of us still carry the nasty habit around as part of our baggage from childhood. Guilt has strengthened at the expense of our self-confidence. Our self-image weakens under the weight of it. Guilt also destroys joy. It makes us worry, fret, and fear.

I met Barbara at a national conference of female executives. A hard worker, she does a lot of traveling for a prestigious company. Barbara earns the kind of money that most women only dream of having. Separated from her parents by half a country, she loves to do special things for them and earmarks some of her generous salary to help ease her parents' lives. Nevertheless, years ago a nasty problem surfaced that made her feel guilty beyond belief.

Her husband became incensed about the money she was sending her parents. He felt she was robbing him of his future and wanted none of the funds funneled to family members. To preserve the peace she agreed with his wishes, but she didn't feel good about it.

On Christmas, she bought her parents a big-screen color television. Her husband went ballistic and selfishly said that would be the last big gift her parents would ever receive because, in his opinion, they weren't worthy of it. That made her tremble. You see, she knew her parents also needed a new car. The one they were driving was two steps away from the auto graveyard. If he was going to get that upset about a television set, she didn't know what to tell him about the car. The thought of having to choose between his anger and the needs of her parents made her sick with guilt and fear.

In her weakness, Barbara had allowed her husband to drive an invisible wedge between her and her parents. His employing one effective method after another over the preceding three years had successfully isolated her from her loved ones. During that time, she had grown tired of fighting him and had been sucked into a whirlpool of co-dependency. Barbara had lost the strength and the will to stand up for what she believed in. The guilt was unrelenting and overpowering.

Throughout the next few months, other unrelated problems surfaced that Barbara could not ignore. Her husband proved to be an unreliable caretaker for her money. Soon, she believed, there wouldn't be enough money in the pot to help anyone.

Out of anger and desperation, she boldly decided to make a stand. As he felt the tide of emotion turning against him, he made one last-ditch appeal. In a moment of bravado, he told her to make a choice. It was either her parents or him. That proved to be his biggest mistake. He had finally tipped the balance of the scales in her parents' favor. The people who loved her and wanted the best for her rose in her respect, while her husband, who was financially and emotionally bleeding her dry, fell. Barbara moved out and filed for divorce the next week. All that guilt and self-reproachfulness, which had drained her for years, dissipated the day she decided to do the right thing.

What about you? First, determine if what you're feeling is real guilt or just someone using guilt to try to make you believe you've committed some offense. If you haven't broken any laws or done anything wrong, why should you feel guilty?

By staying in the clear and always trying not to harm anyone else in thought, word, or deed, we have no need to reproach ourselves. But if the worst happens and we do commit a serious offense, we must work to right the wrong. That is the only way to rid ourselves of guilt. We can try to live with it, but it will drag us down. It will make us disgusted with ourselves and fearful of life. We remove guilt from our lives by acting on it. Remaining passive never cures it and might only intensify the feeling of guilt and dread. Find courage, take action, and right the wrong. When we do that successfully, guilt floats away as effortlessly as a child's helium-filled balloon, lifting our burdens with it.

## DEMOTIVATOR 6: JEALOUSY

What is it you covet the most? What is it that other people have that you don't? There's a great line from the book and movie *Silence of the Lambs*. Hannibal "The Cannibal" Lecter and fledgling FBI agent Clarice Starling discuss what serial killer "Buffalo Bill" covets most. "He covets what he can see, Clarice." That tip leads her to the killer. It can also lead you to answer the question I asked. What is it you covet the most?

We often covet that which we can easily see, but which stands beyond our grasp. No matter how far we extend our arms, we just can't seem to grab hold of what we desire. But that doesn't seem to deter someone else from reaching out and snagging it with ease. As you watch someone else snatching the prize away from your fingertips, you feel envious. Envy is that rush of discontent and ill will that sweeps over you as the other person successfully accomplishes what you could not. Then jealousy moves in as you begin to feel resentment over her good fortune.

Jealousy can be a motivator but it's one of the worst. Nothing good ever comes from jealousy. It breeds insecurity, distrust, possessiveness, and envy. You become watchful of others and very guarded with yourself. You become resentfully suspicious of your rivals.

For more than a decade, I worked beside a news anchor about fifteen years my senior. He arrived on the job one year before I did. I came with less experience, so I received less money. Through the years, both our salaries grew, but his grew substantially larger. Even he admits I worked harder than he did almost all the time. In fact, he used to chide me for it, warning me not to rock the boat because he liked his life just the way it was. Even though my performance was well above industry expectations, he still made more money than I. He got big perks. I got one small perk and even that came with qualifications. I became jealous, which, in turn, made me angry, envious, insecure, and distrustful. I took it out on him. The friendship we once had was in shambles. He began to distrust me because of the way I was acting. Our distance and lack of civility began to show on the air, and could be sensed by some of the viewers at home. My jealousy was beginning to break up a successful anchor team.

One day, a breakthrough came—from a coworker who is also a personal friend of mine. I was sharing with her on a very personal level my feelings of jealousy toward my partner. I told her how I coveted what he had and was angry no one would bestow the riches on me. With one glance, she stopped me dead in my tracks. She explained that my jealousy was inappropriate. She said it was not his fault I didn't have enough goodies in my bag, it was mine. He was a skilled negotiator who knew how to cut a shrewd deal. He demanded more, whereas I, lacking courage, had settled for less. She explained it was all right for me to be angry, but that my anger was misplaced and my jealousy out of line. I should be angry with myself for cutting such a bad deal.

She encouraged me to stop crying over spilt milk and get on with life. Instead of being jealous of my partner, I was to make friends with him and learn from him. I was to find out what he knew that would help me cut a better deal for myself in the future. I put my jealousy aside on that very day.

## DERAIL YOUR DEMOTIVATORS

If I were your local pharmacist, I'd prescribe a healthy dose of confidence to ward off the six deadly demotivators. As your confidence grows and you become more self-assured and in control of your life, these evil enemies of success blow away and scatter like seeds in the wind, enriching your garden with the rich soil of achievement and the budding self-realization of one positive goal after another.

Remember this: *Demotivators are nothing more than figments of your imagination.* They are not real. You invited them into your mind and now it's time to rescind the invitation. Kick them out, posthaste, with courage and confidence.

# CHAPTER 7

## STEP FIVE: PICK UP THE PACE WITH CONFIDENCE

*"A woman is like a tea bag. It's only when she's in hot water that you realize how strong she is."*

—*Nancy Reagan*

Has there ever been a cooler picture of confidence than Marcia Clark on the attack as lead prosecutor in a Los Angeles courtroom? Although her team lost the state's double murder case against former football star O.J. Simpson, she personally emerged as a winner and a hero. Even people who didn't like her grudgingly admired her for the cool and authoritative way in which she handled herself.

Through it all, she maintained an appearance of supreme self-confidence. After the Simpson trial, which ended with a finding of not guilty in the murder of his ex-wife,

Nicole Brown Simpson, and her friend, Ronald Goldman, Clark described her grueling experience as the first true test of her self-esteem.

Clark is a prosecutor with many notches on her belt. Having spent years perfecting her craft, she should have been as confident on the inside as she appeared on the outside. But even with one successful win after another to her credit, apparently something was missing. It wasn't until the Simpson trial, she says, that she pinpointed exactly what it was. Clark, in her first public speech following the conclusion of the trial, was quoted as saying that the Simpson case finally forced her to do something she hadn't done up until that point in her star-studded career. The trial forced her to move forward with confidence, to make her own decisions and stick to them, without seeking approval from others, particularly men.

"I learned once and for all to trust my own instincts, to look within for the final decisions, whether anyone gave me the stamp of approval or not," Clark said in published reports.

Now on the lecture circuit, she urges women to use her experience as an example. She encourages them to trust themselves and their own choices. She teaches them that confidence soars when you strengthen your self-esteem. "Do it the old-fashioned way. You earn it," Clark says. "You earn it by doing it and being conscious of the fact that you're doing it. In essence, you prove it to yourself."

## WHAT IS CONFIDENCE AND WHERE CAN I GET SOME?

A confident woman is very self-assured. She knows, with certainty, that she has exactly what it takes to achieve. Although she may check with her bosses or colleagues to get them to buy in to a change ahead of time or to exchange information that would make her plan more feasible, she doesn't *need* the affirmation of others before proceeding with her ideas and plans. Nor does she require validation to prove that she's on the right track with the choices she makes. In fact, it doesn't matter what the rest of the world thinks. She feels she has the only vote that counts. She believes she can achieve, and that's all there is to it. It's as natural for her as breathing.

Unfortunately, you can't buy a can of confidence at the convenience store. So where do you get the ingredients to mix some up yourself? First, reach deep inside and pull out a healthy measure of self-esteem, which is made up of your positive feelings about yourself. Then add a strong self-image, which is how you see yourself, and stir well. Voilà! That's self-confidence. You enrich the recipe by adding generous dollops of experience, knowledge, and achievement.

Sounds easy, doesn't it? You feel good about yourself and you like what you see. This, in turn, creates a stronger belief in yourself, which is known as confidence. It can take years to cook up some confidence, but when it's ready for serving, it's icing on the cake.

## JUST DO IT!

Achievement is simply the successful accomplishment of the many challenges you face in life. These can be as complex as doing what it takes to ascend to the top management level of your corporation. It can be something as simple as deciding what you want to do this weekend, or as frightening as your husband's cooking up the idea of a dinner party for important business clients on short notice, with you being responsible for the gastronomic delights.

When you know without a trace of doubt you can accomplish the task at hand, you no longer fear the outcome. Confidence is an assurance that overcomes any fears you encounter.

Such is the case of actress Courteney Cox. This star of NBC's hit series, *Friends,* has a different story to tell. Back in 1984, this vivacious brunette had only a couple of TV commercials and soap opera walk-ons to her credit when director Brian De Palma was casting a part for the latest Bruce Springsteen music video of the song "Dancing in the Dark." Cox says she felt overwhelmed when she showed up at the audition and found 300 beautiful females all fighting for the chance to be the young woman Springsteen would pluck from the audience and invite up on stage.

But instead of becoming unnerved and unglued and plunging into self-doubt by worrying if she was pretty enough to win the job, she fell back on her strong self-confidence. When De Palma asked if she had any acting credits, she was ready for the question. She smartly replied, with confidence, "Just two days on *As the World Turns,* but you can change that." He did, and the job propelled her into instant celebrity. The Springsteen video got noticed by the "right" people and became her lucky break. Her confidence had finally caught up with her drive and ambition. The payoff was enormous.

Cox had looked inside herself for strength and brought forward what she had with supreme self-confidence.

## BUT I'M AFRAID TO TAKE CHANCES!

What about you? I know it's hard. Everything frightens us at first when we lack self-confidence, especially the thought of taking that first leap of faith and meeting our first challenge. The first thing we feel is fear. It immobilizes us when what we really need to do is move forward. It's often easier to run away and hide rather than stick our necks out, but hiding is not less dangerous. We're wrong if we think we'll be safer by avoiding confrontation, because we pay an even greater price in the end, as a lack of self-confidence erodes our ability to be a decision-maker and a respected person of value.

If we don't take a chance, we'll never win the prize. So take that first step, and you won't be sorry. The achievement of accepting your first challenge will increase your confidence—immediately.

## EXPAND YOUR KNOWLEDGE

After you take the first big step on the road to achievement, it becomes crucial to keep marching in the right direction. Confident people are knowledgeable. Knowledge feeds our self-confidence as water nourishes a thirsty young plant. The more savvy and erudite we become, the stronger we feel.

The quickest way to bolster sagging self-confidence is to arm ourselves with knowledge. Gather all your facts before you decide how to handle any situation. Keep updated on current events and on the latest information about the subjects that hold your interest. Never stop learning. Use free time wisely. Read every book and magazine you can put your hands on. It doesn't have to cost a cent. The libraries are full of resources. And don't forget those audio-cassette books-on-tape. Even if your car doesn't have a built-in cassette player, use an inexpensive hook-up into the dashboard cigarette lighter for any portable player. Turn off your car radio and use books-on-tape instead—for education, information, and profitable amusement. They can keep you inspired and motivated.

Go back to school, if you so desire. Take a class or attend a seminar. Keep educating yourself. Expand your base of knowledge through a network of new experiences. Knowledge breeds confidence.

I remember talking myself into one of the best jobs of my career when I lacked the knowledge and training needed to back it up. At the time it was a fledgling show, *PM Magazine,* and it looked like fun. Here were two co-hosts, one male, the other female, galloping around the country, doing the most exciting things, sharing magic moments with some of the world's most celebrated people. When I accepted the job, I had a lot of chutzpah but minimal talent. My anchor skills were quite good, but my story-producing ability was severely lacking.

The producers held auditions after a nationwide search for candidates. I was not one of the first ten women they called to Milwaukee to interview for the job, but I was in the next batch of ten on standby status. Bad news came when they offered the job to one woman in the first batch. But fate intervened. She was offered another job in Philadelphia a day later. She took the bigger job, leaving an opening in Milwaukee.

They called for group number two to come forward. I remember my audition that hot July day as if it were yesterday. My self-confidence was zero but my desperation quotient was high. I wanted this job more than life itself. I was willing to square off and physically fight for it if necessary. Thank goodness, it didn't come to that. I was full of bravado and passed the personality test with flying colors. That part has always been my strong suit. They didn't ask me to produce a story, so they didn't spot my weakness. They made the offer. I took it. And then the overwhelming fear set in.

I did not have the confidence to back up my bravado. In three weeks, I reported to my new job and started producing stories. My first efforts were slow and plodding, passable at best. My coworkers were disappointed. They were hoping for an equal partner who could handle her fair share of the load, not someone they would have to guide and teach. I never worked so hard in my life. The more knowledge I acquired about producing and writing, the more confident I became in my storytelling. The job got easier, and, in a short time, I won the respect of my coworkers.

The job enabled me to interview major Hollywood stars and important politicians, and I gained insight and knowledge from each experience. I spent a day in a hospice with a dying woman. I photographed a farmer climbing high on his silo using only his arms, his empty pants legs flapping in the breeze—his legs had been blown off at the hip by a Vietnamese land mine. I accepted the challenge of flying high in a stunt helicopter, 500 feet over the Wisconsin Dells, hanging out the doorless opening with no safety straps, while I interviewed the daredevil performing on a trapeze suspended below me from the body of the 'copter. I learned quickly about life, and my confidence soared because I gained knowledge with each challenge.

Today, I do more than try to succeed. I expect to succeed. I want you to have the expectation of success, too.

## EXPERIENCE IS THE BEST TEACHER

Experience is an important part of the confidence equation. But gaining experience differs from acquiring knowledge. Experience is often more painful, because experience involves confrontation.

When I was a little girl, I loved to embellish stories. "Embellish" is an understatement. What I really did was lie. I learned that a colorful whopper could make me the center of attention, and I loved being center stage. One day I came running home from the schoolyard and told my mother a huge tale of how my girlfriend had run her bicycle into the brick schoolhouse and split open her head. I described with great gusto and gory zeal every bloody moment of the imaginary injury. Oh, you should have seen me. What a remarkable storyteller I was. My mother grew pale.

At the height of my relishing being the bearer of such a delectable tale of horror and gore, my mother did the unexpected. Her first reaction was not to tell me what a good girl I was in hurrying right home to tell her this wonderful, disgusting piece of fabricated news. Instead she called my girlfriend's mother. We all rushed to the schoolyard, and I was pronounced a liar and appropriately punished by the seat of my pants in front of the entire neighborhood. I learned a lot about the importance of truth-telling that day—the hard way. Which is, of course, the same awful way I learned about the dangers of gossiping when I spread nasty lies about the playground favorite in the hopes I could supplant her affection in the hearts of the neighborhood kids. Both true-life experiences negatively affected my budding self-confidence.

Real experience often comes with a painful price tag, and that's why many of us fear it. We can't just read about experience; we have to live it by tasting both the rotten and the sweet things in life and by not blinking in the face of confrontation. It involves putting oneself in situations that others avoid. It's risk versus reward. But really, what have we got to lose? Loss of face, embarrassment, pride? We actually have much more to gain.

Successfully handling conflict puts you in control of any situation. But if you keep avoiding confrontation, you become the big loser in life. First, you lose an opportunity to expand your knowledge, to become a better, smarter, and stronger person. Second, your confidence takes a hit. You can't circumvent challenge and sidestep experience if you want to become confident and self-assured. You must meet them head-on.

Once we begin dealing with conflict in a positive way, we stop fearing it. Like Prosecutor Marcia Clark, we start seeing conflict for what it really is, the best teacher we'll ever have. We actually begin to welcome those stressful situations that give us an opportunity to grow.

## CONFIDENT WOMEN MAKE MISTAKES, TOO

A confident woman makes mistakes just like the rest of the world. The difference between her and others is the way she handles her mistakes.

Nancy Gibson, an attractive local Junior Miss, wanted very much to become Massachusetts Junior Miss. She was bright, though not the scholastic leader in the pageant; talented, though not as talented as some of the others. But Nancy possessed a grace and poise that singled her out. There was one preliminary contest she was confident she could win—the evening gown competition. An endless stairway and several complicated dance steps were the only things standing between her and a scholarship award. At least that's what she thought. At the last moment, the pageant's choreographer had a bright idea: "Let's make the young ladies dance with parasols."

Nancy practiced her twirls and spins and was ready to step into the spotlight. Then disaster struck—right in front of the judges. The girl next to her spun too fast and smacked the parasol right out of Nancy's hands. It landed two feet in front of the judges' table. Humiliated inside but refusing to let it show, Nancy walked up, beamed a gorgeous smile at the judges, mouthed, "Oops," and deftly scooped up the offending prop. With a shrug of her dainty shoulders, Nancy gracefully moved back in position and continued the routine.

That well-timed smile and graceful walk turned a near disaster into an opportunity. An accident of fate had pushed her further into the spotlight. At that moment, she had the judges' full attention, and she made the most of it. She seized the opportunity. In a time of great stress, she radiated confidence. The judges were unanimous in their praise and awarded her a college scholarship as the most graceful and poised Junior Miss in Massachusetts.

## SO, HOW DO YOU GET THERE FROM HERE?

Before we change the way we act, we must change the way we think. This requires a dynamic tool called *affirmation*. It's a positive declaration describing what we want to be and how we choose to live our lives. The technique has been used for centuries by millions of people to beef up their self-confidence. Although it doesn't have the physical power to change anything, it has enormous subjective power to change everything.

You see, it's human nature for each one of us to not only live up to what others expect of us, but also live up to what we expect of ourselves. Every time you use an affirmation, you displace a bad thought with a good one. Your confidence grows as you keep feeding your mind positive thoughts. So create a warehouse of good feelings, and your mind will be able to pull them out of storage automatically at a later date as needed.

An affirmation can be as simple or as complex as you'd like it to be. It's stated in the first person present tense, and it must be very positive. One of my favorites comes from the pages of the Nike handbook. It's the athletic shoe company's famous slogan, "Just Do It." Whenever I feel myself reaching toward indecision or inaction, I modify the slogan and say to myself, "I'm doing it." It works like a charm, every time. That one simple slogan can propel me into a whirl of activity.

Sometimes the most powerful affirmations are the ones we create and design specifically for our needs. A few years ago when I was building my house, a myriad of communication problems arose between me and my builder. We just didn't seem to be on the same page. I would describe what I wanted, but what I often got was not what I had envisioned. I became overwhelmed with petty details and began to sweat the small stuff. I began to fret and to take my problems into the office, which is a major no-no. One day my husband wrote down this affirmation on a 3 x 5 card and pinned it to my bulletin board: "If I can fix it later, it's not a problem now." That was his way of saying everything can be modified or repaired.

That affirmation taught me the value of compromise. I sat down with the builder and found out his problems, we discussed mine, and together we came up with a workable solution. The house cost me slightly more than I planned to pay but much less than it would have if I had retained a lawyer and continued to fight the builder. As a result, I finally got exactly what I wanted. That one, simple affirmation reduced stress and made me feel more confident in bringing successful closure to the situation.

There's only one problem with adopting affirmations as a confidence booster. It's not always easy. Any behavior change is uncomfortable, and boosting one's confidence is no different. But don't get discouraged. It's worth the effort.

The first time you attempt to replace your old destructive thoughts with new, improved ones will probably end in failure. Chances are, you'll reject the new thought because it's unfamiliar. It conflicts with your preconceived notions. But try again. Resistance should give way in the next go-round as your idea gains partial acceptance. Then, after repeated exposures to the new idea, you will assimilate it successfully.

## SEEING IS BELIEVING

You can also enhance your affirmations with visualization—making a mental picture of your goal. Say, for example, your goal is to become a successful entrepreneur. The first thing you do is create a mental picture of yourself owning and operating the business of your choice. This picture should definitely get those juices flowing. It creates desire and fosters the confidence you need to achieve the goal. Keep visualizing it and make it happen.

Visualization provides another valuable service in addition to building confidence. Because it is a form of rehearsal for the real thing, visualization can reveal stumbling blocks along our chosen paths that could keep us from successfully reaching our dreams. By spotting these issues in advance, we can correct problems promptly and proceed without serious consequences. In this case, seeing is definitely believing.

Visualization works for everyday matters as well as for the completion of large goals. If we visualize ourselves cleaning the house or paying the bills, we're more likely to actually dive in and get the nasty deeds done. Even the accomplishment of the little things in life makes us feel more in control and self-assured.

Try this for a visual affirmation: You are a woman singled out from the pack by the strength of your self-confidence. You see yourself seated at the head of a long conference table chairing a meeting of your staff; or perhaps leaning over a subordinate's desk to help him solve a complex production problem. You always remain confident, even in a crisis. Nothing ever seems to ruffle your feathers. You're a woman of firm beliefs who trusts in her own ability. You're reliable. Others feel assured by your presence. You visualize them coming to you to discuss their problems. They believe in your abilities, because you so assuredly believe in your own. Your friends and coworkers never fear telling you a secret, because you are trustworthy.

You picture yourself as a confident woman who is willing to take a risk to get what she wants.

## FILL 'ER UP WITH HIGH-TEST

Too bad I didn't know the power of affirmations years ago, when I botched the biggest interview of my young life. I had retained a high-powered New York City broadcasting agent, who lined me up for a shot at the weekend anchor job at WCBS in New York, owned and operated by the CBS network.

Two days before leaving Milwaukee for New York I began working myself into a frenzy. Every self-doubt came screaming to the surface. My belief that I wasn't good enough for the job butted heads with my overwhelming desire for it. I was as sick as the proverbial dog by the time I boarded the plane for the Big Apple. Worry and self-doubt manifested themselves in a runny nose, a sick stomach, and a pounding headache. Sure that I wasn't good enough for the job, I was turning into a walking billboard advertising the fact.

WCBS had already seen a tape filled with my work. They were already predisposed to like me, or else why would they have called me?

All I needed to do to cinch the deal was walk in, sit down, complete an interview by saying all the things they wanted to hear, and sit at the newsdesk for a brief reading of the news on camera—all things I had done with success many times before. So why was this time difficult? Because at that stage in my career I had no confidence in myself and my abilities, that's why.

Things grew even worse once I entered the hallowed halls of CBS in Manhattan. My fears and self-doubts escalated. They took another hit when I was made to cool my heels. Waiting in a foyer, I watched the world walk by for the next two hours. Eventually, a secretary approached, and I thought, "This is it." My stomach flipped and I actually became nauseated. But the secretary merely wanted to inform me of a further delay and ask if I'd like to go to the cafeteria for something to drink. I stumbled gratefully along behind her, and when we reached our destination she turned on her heel and left me without even a goodbye.

Morosely I took a seat at the back of the cafeteria and once again began practicing the answers to every question anyone could possibly ask me. I tried to summon up any vestige of confidence, but I was tapped out. For another two hours I sat there, feeling like a bar girl waiting for a john to buy her a drink. In my own mind, I was outclassed and out of place. I didn't belong in this group of winners. They certainly wouldn't let anyone who was important to them sit and stew like this.

One famous face after another walked by. I was startled to see *60 Minutes'* correspondent Morely Safer having a nosh across the cafeteria from me. He nodded hello, then got up and walked away. I was tempted to stop him and ask him if what I was going through was some cruel CBS ritual of torture designed to test a job applicant's ability to withstand stress. If so, I was failing miserably.

Finally, the dreaded summons came. By then I had convinced myself that all was lost. Instead of walking into this important interview with strength, I was an emotional mess.

As the man in charge asked me to talk about myself, I did the unforgivable. Already frenzied with self-doubt, I began describing my weak points and how I planned to overcome them. The interview went downhill from there. This was my shot at the big time and I was expertly shooting myself in the foot. In spite of my embarrassing interview, he told me he liked my work very much and added that I was a wonderful story producer. Then came the moment of truth. He put me on the anchor set to test my abilities to broadcast the news live. It was the worst moment of my life. To be an anchor you must be confident above all else. I was anything but. At that moment I couldn't have sold a story even if it wore a bargain-basement price tag.

The interviewer explained what I had expected to hear right from the start. He was not going to give me the job. But it had nothing to do with my ability. He felt my work spoke for itself; I was a very strong reporter with potential for anchoring, but—and it was a big but—he felt I didn't have enough confidence for the job, that I would be eaten alive on the mean streets of New York City. He was right.

Having confidence is all about believing in yourself so you're not afraid to show them the stuff of which you're really made.

You don't need to be a television personality to possess special qualities that make you feel confident. Each of us has such qualities. Some are easy to pick out; others are hidden. No matter how you feel about yourself right now, understand that you are unique and bring special gifts to the table. We need to understand what those gifts are and how to best use them to feel confident about ourselves.

Confidence is also about not being afraid to take a risk to capture a reward. If I had remained powerful at that job interview in New York instead of exposing my low self-esteem and poor self-image, I would never have been left cooling my heels. I should have asserted myself and demanded respect. They wanted a fighter, but I showed them I had little fire in my belly for that. They wanted me to stand up for myself and demand the proper treatment. I failed the confidence test. I let myself down by giving them too much control over my life. They moved on and found someone else who didn't need to ask for permission before taking action. I was left sad, disappointed, and filled with weakness.

## AVOID THE PERFECTION TRAP

As you work to become more confident, strive to be the best you can be, but don't become obsessive about achieving perfection. Women who strive to be flawless and socially acceptable give the illusion of self-assuredness. To see them in action, you would never believe they suffer from a shortage of self-confidence.

A good example of this is former television news anchor and network correspondent Jessica Savitch—the golden girl who appeared to have everything but the strong belief in herself necessary to keep her star shining.

Savitch was a successful network anchor at the age of

thirty-one, loved by the viewing public, resented by many of her peers. She traveled the fastest track of all in the hectic, hard-driving world of television news. Professionally, she was at the zenith of her career. Personally, she was plagued by drugs, depression, and personal disasters, apparently fueled by low self-esteem and a poor self-image.

I met Savitch two times during my first twenty years in broadcasting. The first was in 1979, when I was a fledgling anchor myself in Scranton, Pennsylvania. Savitch was receiving an honorary doctorate from her alma mater, Ithaca College. I called her up and asked if I could have a one-on-one interview with her even though I was affiliated with a rival television network. She graciously accepted. I was nervous. She was everything I desired to be. During the interview I found her warm, charming, funny, responsive, and very engaging. I walked away entranced, thinking I had found my role model.

Then I began to hear the stories through the television grapevine that she was not the confident woman and consummate professional she appeared to be. I was told she was shallow, and what she lacked in talent and skill she made up for with chutzpah and a unique talent for marketing herself. As a result, the public couldn't get enough of Jessica Savitch. But this created headaches for the big network bosses. Savitch was like a human time bomb waiting to explode. All her fears and lack of confidence kept building up inside her, and instead of doing the positive things necessary to correct a situation and turn it around, she made one misstep after another. She turned to drugs and fell into and out of depression.

Years after our first meeting, I ran into Savitch again. I was working in Milwaukee when I was chosen to fly to New York City to participate on a panel with newswomen from across the country. I was flattered by the honor and excited when I heard Savitch would be the moderator of our panel. I couldn't wait to see her again now that her star had ascended to the very top of TV heaven. However, what I witnessed that day both astounded and appalled me.

An emaciated-appearing Savitch came striding into the roomful of wanna-be Jessicas, surrounded by an entourage of what appeared to be yes-men and women. She was snapping her fingers and barking out orders. It appeared to me that she was using the presence of the entourage to increase her self-importance. The woman I had admired for years was behaving like a prima donna.

As I sat there, I wondered what could have happened to this woman to alter her so much. Savitch's luster was gone. There was no fire in her eyes, no life. To me, she appeared a painful picture of insecurity, a woman who seemed to be grabbing for any handhold to save herself from falling from grace. Where was the seemingly self-assured woman I had met back in 1979, the woman who was on her way to the top, the woman who told me she wanted to be perfect?

There is no substitute for self-confidence. Drugs and alcohol are not the answer. Don't be tempted. Instead, see yourself as a strong, capable woman who doesn't need crutches to support herself through life.

## CONFIDENT WOMEN MAKE THEIR OWN MAGIC

The time for waiting is over. The magic fairy is not going to arrive in a swirl of stardust and tap you three times on the head with her wand to make you confident. You have to make it happen. Start shaping yourself today into a strong woman who knows without a doubt that she can achieve her goals and find success.

# CHAPTER 8

# STEP SIX:
# COMMUNICATE CAREFULLY

*"Listening, not imitation, may be the sincerest form of flattery."*
—Dr. Joyce Brothers

Remember the television series *Wild, Wild West* and how luscious Bob Conrad looked in the persona of James West? Not only was he terrific in performing his role as America's first Secret Service agent, but he is also a born communicator, as I found out when I met him on a media movie junket. A junket is a promotional event in which a movie studio sends reporters, all expenses paid, to an elegant hotel in an exciting city, like L.A. or Chicago, to interview the stars of its latest flick.

It took me only minutes after meeting him to realize that actor Robert Conrad possesses all the qualities necessary for successful communication. He's warm, friendly, and engaging. He presents a powerful self-image and has a well-developed sense of humor, which he uses liberally. In even the briefest of encounters he works to establish mutual understanding. And that, after all, is the secret to good communication.

The movie Conrad was pushing turned out to be a very forgettable film that also starred Sean Connery. The most noteworthy thing about the entire film is that it's the first time we see the former 007 without his hairpiece. Connery plucks it off his head in one of the final scenes as he jumps from a plane.

I was scheduled to meet with both stars in a plush hotel room in Chicago. At the center of the room stood a king-sized chair, an opulent chair, no doubt chosen with the regal Connery in mind. He would have looked like *The Man Who Would Be King* of a rich country in that ornate, obviously expensive chair. Reporters were assigned much simpler seats. I took my simple seat with alacrity and eagerly awaited the arrival of the world's classiest male star.

When the door opened, in strode a star of a smaller stature, Bob Conrad. Brimming with confidence and heaps of good self-esteem, he walked over to me, made direct eye contact, clasped my hand warmly, and then gave it a hearty handshake. He was direct and forthright as he explained to me that Sean had called it quits for the day because he wasn't feeling well. "Would an interview with me be sufficient?" he asked.

Then he proceeded to do the most amazing thing, something I never saw an interview subject do before or since. Conrad began asking *me* questions about *me*. He seemed really interested. I was absolutely stunned. Definitely the charmer, he quickly dissipated any disappointment I had about the loss of the interview with Connery—which was exactly what Conrad had in mind.

As he worked to establish rapport and an air of mutual understanding between us, he was making me forget the Connery no-show while increasing his chances for a successful interview. By the time we were ready to start taping, I knew where he was coming from and he knew the same about me. Together we formed the ground rules for our interview. I let him know nothing was sacred. He was up front and honest.

The crowning moment in good communication came when Conrad took the chair reserved for Connery. It could have been an awkward scene because Conrad, you see, is not as big as he appears on television. The heroics of James West make him appear taller and often larger-than-life. But Conrad is a much shorter man than you'd expect to find filling those big shoes. And when he hopped into that immense chair, his feet did not reach the floor.

He laughed heartily. "Oh great," he joked, as the camera began to roll. "Here I am being interviewed by Miss Milwaukee, and my feet don't even touch the floor!"

Rather than communicating embarrassment at not being able to fill Connery's chair, he used humor to make me laugh with him instead of at him, while gesturing to the crew that he needed another chair, pronto.

A more suitable chair was brought in. The interview continued. It proved to be a big success for both of us.

## COMMUNICATION INVOLVES MUTUAL UNDERSTANDING

We can all learn a lesson from Robert Conrad and use smart communication techniques to better our lives and improve the many difficult situations we find ourselves in, often on a daily basis. The key to good communication is very simple.

It begins with a strong foundation of mutual understanding. To be understood is one of the deepest needs an individual has. We all share a basic desire to have other people understand us. We want to be able to reach a mutual understanding with another person and have both parties walk away satisfied, which significantly increases our odds of getting our message across and receiving someone else's input.

An important note: This doesn't mean we have to agree with the ideas and opinions of the other person. It just means we need to understand with clarity the message he or she is communicating to us.

## WE COMMUNICATE ON FOUR LEVELS

Good communicators know how to listen as well as talk. As author Stephen Covey says, we must seek first to understand, then to be understood. What he means is that we must concentrate fully on what the other person is saying, rather than selecting only what pleases us or fits our preconceived ideas. That's not an easy thing to do when you consider that most of us speak approximately 125 words a minute, while we can think at the rate of 400 to 600 words a minute.

Listening also helps us determine the level of communication. I've been told we humans communicate on four different levels.

1. Level One is the *social* level. Included in this category are our more superficial relationships, such as the person you pass in the hall at work every day. You look at each other, nod, and say, "Hi."
2. Level Two brings us up a notch to the *casual-personal* category. This is where we bump into someone we

know and ask her something such as, "How are the children doing in school?"

3. The next level, Level Three, is *information sharing.* This is where we get to the nuts and bolts of whatever matter we're discussing. "So, the price of the house will include those kitchen cabinets and the Corian countertop?"

4. This brings us to Level Four, a place of *open and honest communication.* It involves a genuine sharing of feelings and opinions on a much deeper level than sharing information. This is the level at which emotions are felt and expressed. "I'm so sorry you had to put your dad in a nursing home. I know you wanted to keep him in his own home as long as possible. It was a tough call."

To be an active listener, we must pay attention to the conversation and quickly ascertain on what level the other person is trying to communicate with us. Let's say she's talking on Level Four, open and honest communication, and you are listening on Level One, social. Chances are you won't hear her message, because your mind is racing in some other direction.

Here's the scenario:

Toni passes Sally in the hall at work. Toni's got her mind on a great party to which she's been invited. In her Level One state she utters, "Hi, how's it going?" She really doesn't want an answer; she is just trying to be polite. Sally answers, "My mom just died. I'm on my way to see my dad." She's definitely on Level Four.

Toni answers, "Oh, I'm sorry. I guess that means you won't be going to Bob's party tonight. Too bad. They say it's going to be really great. I'm all excited. Can't wait to go!" Toni drones on cheerfully in her Level One state. She wasn't actively listening on the proper level and didn't feel the impact of the other woman's grief; therefore, she failed to respond appropriately.

One more thing to keep in mind is that men and women seem to start their communication on different levels. Throughout my years of interviewing and reporting, I've noticed that men seem to feel most comfortable starting on the *social* level, working their way up through *casual-personal* to *information sharing*. We hardly ever see a man jump right in at Level Four, *open and honest communication*.

But that's not the way we women work. We usually go right for Level Four with all the gusto we can muster, a method of communication that can make a grown man squirm.

Here's the proof. You've just been to the doctor, and she's decided your female plumbing needs a little work—a D&C is in order. You need to go to your male boss and ask for some time off. Instead of just saying, "I need two days off for a small surgical procedure," you dive right in and give him all the grisly details of your heavy menstrual flow. Ladies, that is too much open and honest information.

From this day forward, do your best to listen intently and to immediately determine on what level the other person is speaking. Move to that level as quickly as possible. This is the proper place to increase mutual understanding and establish rapport.

## COMMUNICATING WITH A CAPTIVE AUDIENCE

Nothing drove this point home to me more than a visit to the Women's Reformatory in Marysville, Ohio, in 1996. This is not a prison full of minor offenders and lawbreakers. It's a hard-core, gritty world far from the one in which most of us live, a world filled with felons, prostitutes, thieves, drug addicts, and killers.

I was called to the prison to share my "Ten Steps to Success" program with the women inmates in the drug recovery program. The director asked me to deliver a heavy emphasis on self-esteem issues. Most of the people I told about my upcoming adventure were puzzled.

"What in the world are you going to tell women behind bars about finding success?" they asked me. I answered them honestly by admitting I just didn't know how to address this highly extraordinary group, but I was eager to try.

The ride to the prison seemed endless. It gave me nearly two hours to reflect on how to communicate to this captive audience my message of finding success and developing leadership skills. I really didn't know what to expect. Would the women welcome me or would I find them a hostile audience?

As I traveled up a long, winding road that cut through naked cornfields, I caught my first sight of the massive fortress. Looking more like a grim, battle-scarred castle, it stood out from the landscape, an immense holding pen rimmed by fences topped with barbed wire.

The prison didn't need bars to make it appear rigid and foreboding. The coldness intensified as I passed through one metal detector after another to gain entrance. As I walked on to the building housing the drug recovery program, I felt fear, dread, and misery. My head began to pound as I wondered, for the last time, what I was doing here and what message I could possibly deliver to help these imprisoned women.

But that sorrowful picture changed as I walked into the room where I was to give my talk. My eyes widened in surprise as beautiful, intensely colorful hand-painted pictures leapt out from the drab walls. Each picture told a story of hope and promise. Some included biblical sayings offering inspiration; others were original poems written from the heart of the women inmates involved in the recovery program.

The hands that had spent hours painting these murals now reached out from everywhere to welcome me. I felt the coldness ebbing away in the warmth of the overwhelming reception I got from these women who were so desperate to hear a message of hope and strength.

I opened up our communication at Level Three—information sharing—because the circumstances of our meeting propelled us beyond any social or casual chatter. Soon I realized that these women behind bars are not so different from you and me. They started out in life just like anyone else, with the same hopes, dreams, and expectations. They played with dolls and went to school, but unlike you and me, they had something go terribly wrong in their lives. Lacking in self-esteem and personal leadership values, many of them listened with trust to the wrong people. Imprisonment is what they had to show for it.

Most of the women I talked with that day have children on the outside. They admit they made some serious mistakes and poor choices in the past. But they want to become stronger and independent so that when they leave their jail cells and return to their old neighborhoods, they can support and protect their children both emotionally and financially. They also want to have the courage to stay away from the bad influences that led to their incarceration. For most of them, that means drugs and the wrong men, the vices of choice for many women who lack a strong self-image and self-respect.

The women I met in Marysville prison are a far cry from strong women who stand up for their beliefs and principles. The complete opposite of feminists, many of them had become willing pawns in someone else's game. They were looking to me for some advice and encouragement to start making smart choices, to become leaders instead of followers.

I delivered my message that day, but only after doing everything I possibly could to ensure that it would be received and understood by my audience, such as asking them lots of questions.

## BE THE ONE ASKING THE QUESTIONS

Asking appropriate questions deepens the quality of your communication. Become an expert at gathering information while you gain the other person's trust and respect. Asking questions sets the scene for sharing. While you listen, you learn. And always remember this important fact: "She who asks the questions controls the communication."

Learn how to ask probing, open-ended questions. An open-ended question is one that requires more than a yes or no answer. The best way to learn this technique is to try it on children. Throughout my years of broadcasting, I've learned that children are the toughest people to interview. We must phrase our questions very carefully or something like this happens:

"Do you like Santa Claus?"

"Yes."

"Is Santa going to come tonight?"

"Yes."

"Are you going to leave cookies and milk out for him?"

"Yes."

Here's a better way to ask the questions:

"Santa's coming tonight? What will he look like when he pops down your chimney? What are you going to leave out for the big guy to snack on tonight?"

If you can successfully master kids, you can master the art of open-ended questions with adults. The most important lesson I've learned on this subject over the years is to never ask a person a question that could be answered with a simple yes or no. Closed questions may succeed in extracting basic information, but they often produce little else. By asking an open-ended question, we're forcing the other person to analyze the issue at hand, express an opinion about it, or interpret information.

Instead of saying, "Did you finish the report as scheduled?" try, "What information in the report needs further action?"

Always ask a lot of open-ended questions. The more we know about the people with whom we're communicating, the more effective we become in asking questions that encourage others to dig deep inside themselves and tap their creativity.

Try also to consider each person's personality style when framing a question. If you know someone is the thoughtful type, use that information to frame your question: "What do you *think* we should do to clear up this mess?" If the person is an emotional type, try the same question this way: "What do you *feel* is the best way to clear up this mess?" Or if the person is a control freak: "What are you going to *do* to help clear up this mess?"

Also, take a good look at the person who's trying to communicate with you. Listen carefully to the words she uses, her tone of voice, and how she delivers her message. Listen for what a person is *not* saying as well as concentrating intently on the words she is speaking. Try to read her emotions and attitudes. Evaluate her body language. Is it open and welcoming, or closed and guarded?

Body language is a powerful communication tool. How we stand, sit, hold our arms, and cross our legs are often more potent than the words spilling from our lips. Body language can kill our message as effectively as it can enhance it. The experts say nonverbal communication makes up an amazing 58 percent of a person's total message. Tone of voice, which is the *way* we say things, accounts for 35 percent. The actual words we speak make up only 7 percent of the total message.

## WHAT KINDS OF SIGNALS ARE YOU SENDING?

It's time to find out what you're communicating about yourself to others. Do they see you as strong and confident as you want to appear? The following "doughnut test" often proves most revealing.

Take a look at the worksheet on the next page. I don't know who invented this little game, but I took this "test" at a seminar once, and I was astonished to see before me, in black and white, exactly what I was communicating about myself to others.

This test works best with a group of people you barely know, because people who know you intimately tend to write things about you from their knowledge of you rather than from your success or failure in communicating what's inside you.

Here's how to proceed:

1. Make a photocopy of the next page, with enough copies so everyone in the group gets one.
2. Sit in a circle.

# Name _____

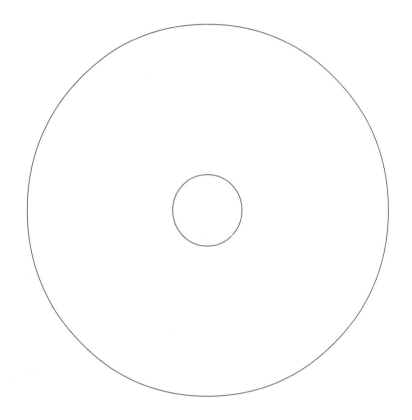

3. Each person writes his or her name at the top of one sheet and then passes it to the next person.

4. Each sheet continues being passed to every person in the group before it comes full circle back to its originator.

5. As each sheet goes around the circle, its recipient takes a good look at the person whose name is at the top of it and writes down, in the fat part of the doughnut, the first adjective that comes to mind to describe that person.

   For example, does she appear strong, intelligent, serious, or fun? Is he looking solemn, thoughtful, jovial, or stern? Take the most dominant characteristic and write it down.

6. Keep the sheets circulating until everyone has had a chance to add his or her own adjective to each person's sheet.

7. When your own comes back to you, take a hard look at the words on it. They reflect a true picture of what you're communicating to others.

The first time I participated in this exercise, I remember how disappointed I was when my doughnut came back to me. I had hoped for adjectives such as strong, smart, sincere, and respected. What I got was a page full of cute descriptive words like perky, ebullient, and fun. I became severely distressed. Is this the message I was sending out to the rest of the world—a world in which communicating a strong first impression is essential to success? I vowed that day to make the changes necessary in life to make future doughnut tests come out the way I wanted them to—filled with strength and respect.

This is where the middle of the doughnut comes in. If you like the outcome of the exercise and are satisfied with the results, take the adjective you like best and write it in the center. Use it as a reminder that you're on track and comfortable with the message you are sending out. But if you hate the adjectives assigned to you, as I did, simply choose a new, stronger adjective for yourself and boldly place it in the center. That day I chose "intelligent" over "well liked."

Keep the completed test in your home, office, or DayTimer. Use it as a reminder of where you are now and where you want to end up. When you put your new adjective in writing, you plant the seed that grows into a new you, and you allow and encourage change to happen.

Although I have taken the test many times since, the first time was the most important. My change did not occur overnight, but my progression from being seen as a "perky, fun" woman to being recognized as a woman of substance and intelligence finally occurred. What I chose to project amazingly became both a perception and a reality.

## PERCEPTION IS REALITY

Whenever you walk into an interview, step up to a podium, or stride into an everyday situation, make sure people perceive you as being courageous and confident. This perception will immediately grab people's attention and make your job of communicating with them easier. They will perceive your strength and respect your healthy self-image. The perception of you as an effective communicator will quickly become reality, and you'll have no problem with people not understanding the messages you're sending to them.

A strong self-image paves the way for the all-important foundation of mutual respect, which leads to effective communication. Failure to project a strong self-image often brings trouble to your door.

I was twenty-one, and old enough to know better, when I decided to bring out what I thought was the "real me." There I was, all decked out in a skimpy halter top, a mini-skirt, and platform shoes—the utmost in fashion. Well, that look may have worked on a fashion house runway in Paris, but it failed miserably in the workplace. Inside, I was a good girl filled with old-fashioned values and strong morals, but that wasn't the message I was sending to the rest of the world. I looked cheap and inviting, and because of it I didn't lack for invitations. However, the quality of those invitations often matched the quality of the clothes I was barely wearing. I was a walking billboard, sending out a message that wasn't me.

I dressed that way because I lacked self-confidence and self-esteem. In my warped sense of reality, I had noticed that the more I revealed of myself, the more people paid attention to me. People began staring at me and smiling. What I realized too late was the meaning of their little tight-lipped smiles. Many of them were embarrassed for me. No one had the guts to tell me what I was doing was wrong—except my mother, and of course, I didn't listen to *her*. I just thought it was Mom being Mom.

I found out I was wrong, in the most painful way. An executive at work whom I had admired for a very long time stopped by my desk one day. Softly he asked me out to lunch. I was thrilled. He was handsome, kind, successful, and, I thought, available. I was wrong on almost all counts. I had heard he and his wife were no longer together, so before accepting his invitation, I asked about her. He confirmed the story and said his marriage was over. We drove to the restaurant in my car. I always like being in control, even when it appears I'm out of control. We had a lovely lunch, but I soon realized he spent more time looking at my halter top than into my eyes. I began to grow increasingly uncomfortable with some of the things he was saying. It was becoming obvious to me that he had gotten the wrong impression about me. I wanted to leave. He suggested taking the wheel of my car for the drive back to the office. He was very forceful about it, so I slid into the passenger seat and he got behind the wheel.

All of a sudden he made his move. He pounced on me, right there in the parking lot of the restaurant. He forced my head back with a sloppy, wet kiss. I told him to stop but he wouldn't listen. His hand reached into my halter top and grabbed my breast and squeezed. I was astounded, alarmed, and frightened. I didn't know what was going to happen next as I worked furiously to free myself from his grip.

I was saved that day by the most amazing coincidence. It seems that this man's wife, from whom he was *not* separated, happened to be sitting in a different part of the same restaurant. She happened to turn her head at a crucial moment and look out the restaurant window into my car. When she saw what was occurring, she ran to my car, opened the passenger door and squeezed into the front seat beside me. First she slapped him and then she slapped me. I looked straight into her eyes and saw the pain I had unwittingly caused. During her tirade, I realized this was not the first time she had caught him pressing his attentions on another woman. She called me cheap, and I couldn't blame her. I was mortified and wanted to die.

I demanded they both leave my car, and I drove away, shaken and appalled that I had sent out the wrong message. What he had done was wrong, and he had no right to do so, because I never explicitly invited him to touch me. But I learned a valuable lesson that day about sending out subtle, or not-so-subtle, messages. I felt dirty and cheap.

I went home, took off all my clothes and burned them in the fireplace. I went through my closet and at great personal expense replaced my entire wardrobe. It was money I couldn't afford to spend, but there was no question in my mind that it had to be done. Like a phoenix, I rose from the ashes sprouting fine new feathers. Today, I always dress appropriately for the occasion to make sure my appearance doesn't send out a different message than the one I intend to communicate.

## WORD POWER

Be on the lookout for people with weak self-images who use words to attack rather than confront. Whenever they feel threatened, they quickly reach into their verbal arsenal and pull out hurtful words designed to skewer another person's self-confidence. It's important to realize the power words have to hurt others, so don't ever take the responsibility lightly. The experts say it takes thirteen compliments to counteract every negative thing we say to somebody. Think about this the next time you might be tempted to use clever words to cut down someone else.

We have the power to wound, hurt, and crush someone else's feelings every time we open our mouths. That's why it's imperative to communicate from a position of strength. People who possess low self-esteem often feel stronger by hitting weak people right where it hurts. But when you're riding high with self-respect and confidence, you don't do business that way. Instead, you seek out the positive in every situation and treat other people with respect. Mutual respect opens the doors of communication and increases the chances that another person will accept your ideas and beliefs.

While working in Pittsburgh in 1994, I was approached by a woman who apparently needed a transfusion of self-confidence. She was a hurtful person who used her communication skills to bring other people down to her level. She met her match the day she met me.

It was a charitable event and I was making a personal appearance, which means I was giving a speech without charging for my time. All I expected was a thank-you, but what I got felt like a kick in the teeth. The individual came striding over to me, all smiles and cheer, appearing warm and pleasant. She did all the right things. She reached for my hand and moved in to establish rapport. She leaned in closely to my ear but spoke loudly enough for everyone at the table to hear.

"Donna, I'm so happy you're with us today." So far so good, but she went on. "I remember the last time I went to one of your speeches, I so looked forward to the event. And then, there you were, dressed all in black. I was so disappointed. You looked terrible, just terrible. Black is your worst color. You obviously need to have your colors done by a professional consultant."

That's when I turned to her, smiled, grabbed her hand warmly, looked her straight in the eyes, and said, "I've had my colors done three times, and I'm definitely a winter. Black is my best. But thank you for coming over and saying hello." I dismissed her with aplomb. However, this gal was not one to take a rebuff lightly. In a few minutes, she came back for more.

"I'd like to apologize for what I said before, and I hope you're not upset with me. I've been thinking it over, and yes, you're right, black is your color. I guess my judgment was affected because you looked so bad that day." Then she droned on, "You had these horrible bags under your eyes and your complexion looked sallow. I was so disappointed in your appearance. Can't you see how I could have made a mistake like that?" She grinned.

If her mission was to cut the television anchor down to size by drop-kicking her from her self-appointed pedestal, the woman failed miserably. You could hear a pin drop at the table as the other women waited to see how I would handle this latest assault.

"You asked me if I was upset with you. I am not at this moment, but if you continue with this negative assault, I will become angered, and that's something you don't want to see." Then I smiled and said a brisk "Good-bye," turned my back on her, and resumed my conversation with the other women seated at my table. I politely took a stand that day and refused to buckle under her assault.

When you work on television, people take shots at you all the time. I'm not sure exactly why, but for some reason people say things to me, a person they don't even know, that they wouldn't dare say to their family and friends. I guess they think I have the hide of an armadillo and can roll up into a ball when hurt, so their barbs won't pierce my skin. Those people don't seem to understand that I have feelings too, feelings that can be hurt.

However, after years of being in the public eye, I can easily tell the difference between someone kindly offering me criticism and someone else who is lobbing verbal grenades at me. If this person had just come over to me and said, "I don't think black is your color. Have you ever checked? Can I be of assistance?" I would have responded in a much different manner. I would have been kind even if she unintentionally said something insensitive or unkind about me in front of the other seven women at the table.

The question here is intent. I won't allow myself to be verbally attacked by an insecure or mean-spirited person who delights in using words as weapons.

## TIMING IS EVERYTHING

Even the most perfectly framed message can fall flat if it's delivered at the wrong time. I found that out the hard way when I became fed up on a location shoot and decided I wasn't going to take it anymore. This was 1981, during a *PM Magazine* taping at Milwaukee's famous Summerfest, an annual event.

My videographer and I were surrounded by hundreds, possibly even thousands, of onlookers as we were trying to get the show videotaped and in the can. The crowd didn't mean to be disruptive and discourteous; they were simply having fun. As far as they were concerned, the taping of a television show on the Summerfest grounds was just one more amusement for their pleasure. Every time we rolled the tape, something negative would happen. Cheers, jeers, and even beer were being hurled at us, but still we persevered. Finally, after several busted takes of a particularly troublesome monologue, I was determined not to let anything or anyone get in the way of a successful take. If we got it right this time, we could push on and out of the teeming masses of Milwaukeeans.

I began my countdown to set the audio level on the microphone, "Ten-nine-eight-seven-six-five-four-three-two-one." I took a deep breath and began to walk forward. At that moment, I felt a hand reach out from the crowd behind me—an extremely frightening thing to have happen in a mob atmosphere. Determined to keep going, I nevertheless fully intended to communicate a good, clear message for everyone to leave me alone so I could get my job done. In an effort to fend off the perceived attack from behind, I moved my right arm forward as unobtrusively as possible and then rammed it back behind me hard, right into the solar plexus of the person who had grabbed me.

All at once, the crowd gasped. People stared at me with astonishment and derision, as if I were some bug crawling up the wall. Even my videographer stopped shooting and rose up over his camera, looking stunned and frozen at a point beyond me. Slowly, I turned around and followed the gaze of the crowd to the individual lying on the ground behind me.

In my desire to communicate a strong message to be left alone, I had pushed a child. Moreover, he was a child with a disability, who was at that moment lying on his back like a turtle, leg braces in the air, working hard to right himself. I couldn't believe what I had done.

I had sent a strong message, all right, but at the wrong time. I was crying as I bent down to scoop up the child. His mother came running over. She was also crying. I apologized until I thought my heart would break. She was crying too, but from embarrassment that her son had ruined a piece of work that I was trying so desperately to complete. Amazingly, she was apologizing to me. She realized I had become concerned by the unruliness of the crowd, and she was sorry her child had frightened me into my inappropriate action. Of course, I refused to let her and her son take the blame.

Fortunately, the boy wasn't hurt, and he giggled and laughed as if my over-protective behavior were part of a silly game. He and I both learned important lessons that day. Mine was that a poorly timed message has no chance for success.

To keep disasters like that from happening to you, scope out the situation carefully and choose the right timing and emotional climate in which to communicate your message. Examine the other person's facial features and body language. Does she look as though the time is right for her to hear what you have to say? The better the mood the other person is in, the more likely it is that you may get a positive response.

It's like asking your supervisor or manager if you can take Tuesday off because there's something personal you need to get done. Study her before you crawl out on the limb with your request. Look at her body language and listen to her tone of voice. If she's upbeat and receptive, chances are favorable that you could get what you desire. If not, wait a while to increase your chance for a successful outcome.

## BRIDGING THE COMMUNICATION GAP WITH MEN

For years we women have been complaining that men don't take us seriously. We feel our suggestions aren't appreciated and our advice is not valued.

The most important thing a woman can do when communicating with a man is to be direct. Realize that men and women communicate differently. Deborah Tannen, author of *You Just Don't Understand: Men and Women in Conversation*, points out that men use language to establish status and preserve independence; women use language to establish intimacy. Women, for example, are seldom as direct as men, partly because they are uneasy with giving direct orders and prefer to reach consensus. This can cause problems in the office because the indirect approach often makes men feel manipulated.

Often, it's not what women are saying but how we say it. If we want to step off on the right foot when communicating with a member of the male sex, we must establish credibility immediately and maintain our integrity throughout the entire relationship. We must be direct. This garners the respect of men and the admiration of women.

But there's something more important to know to successfully communicate with the male gender. Women and men process information differently. Women are global thinkers. Men are compartmentalized.

This difference often creates a major communication barrier. Ask a woman how she feels about an issue and you often get a complicated answer. Because she thinks globally, she looks at the big picture. How will this issue affect my family, my workplace, the environment, peace, harmony, and racial injustice? As she processes all this information, a woman could appear scatterbrained. She sees a hundred different ways to deal with the issue at hand, and she's not sure which is the best way. Ask the man the same question and he usually zeros in directly on the main point. He doesn't digress or equivocate. He makes a decision, right or wrong, and lives with it.

My husband is a great example of compartmentalized thinking. He is a visionary in the field of management consulting. He has brought companies successfully into the future and made others cash cows with his good advice. While he thinks globally in business, I have watched him struggle with compartmentalized thinking on a personal level, such as when we talk to each other on our mobile car phones. When I'm driving, I can pick up the phone to talk to him while I'm moving out at sixty-five miles per hour, listening to the radio, reading my directions, and concentrating on where I'm going. It doesn't work that way for him. When he's talking with me on the car phone, in the middle of a sentence I hear, "Oh-oh." I know exactly what that means. He's missed his exit. It happens more often than not, because he's in that special compartment reserved for talking to me. If he's concentrating on what I'm saying, I fill up his compartment, and between that and trying to drive carefully, there's no room left for him to process the information about exit signs. This degree of focus is useful to men in certain situations, but not in all situations.

Learn to use these differences in communication to help each other rather than feel frustrated by them. Because I'm a global thinker, I have to be careful not to appear disjointed, flighty, or impractical to someone I'm trying to win over to my message. I have learned from my husband how to be more direct. I found out how to tunnel my vision somewhat and step into a compartment to filter out distractions. As for my husband, the world he sees has grown larger since he met me. He has opened his vision to a host of new experiences. He has also learned to trust that intangible thing called my "woman's intuition." He's seen it in action and welcomes the input while he's making his decisions. It is my belief that women's intuition is really a combination of things, but mostly it's knowledge gleaned from being open to multiple experiences and subtle clues. It's common sense combined with global thinking.

If you want to get a man's attention and make him really listen to what you have to say, do so by moving him into the right compartment. This is crucial. Confronting your boss with a list full of questions just as he's leaving for an important financial meeting is not likely to be good timing. He's got other things on his mind. He's in a different compartment from the one you want him in. When men are stressed they become even more compartmentalized.

You need to bring him out of that compartment, not encourage him to retreat further into it.

Talk to him first in a very casual way. "Boy, that financial preparation must have been tough." Then, by asking one question after another, gradually lead him to where you want him to go. Be positive and upbeat. Make him excited to enter the new compartment. "Well, I've got a terrific proposal here that you're going like!"

If you feel you're not making an impact, take another route. Write your information in a memo and give it to him to study. Set up a time when you and he can talk again after he's had the opportunity to read your information. By the time you get to that meeting, he should have a compartment there with your name on it. You will then have his full attention.

Another problem that stifles communication between the sexes is that men often use a more combative approach, while women prefer a less confrontational style. He thinks he's being helpful when he takes your idea and then proceeds to punch holes in it, often in front of your coworkers. Your feelings are not spared as your idea is dissected and then torn apart piece by piece. Your spirit sags and you become defensive about what's left of your once brilliant idea. You feel personally attacked, and instead of making a few changes and fighting for what you believe in, you drop the whole thing.

Before you lose confidence and scrap your idea, you must view his attack differently. Don't take it personally. Most men have a focused, sequential perspective, and when that's combined with a combative nature, things like this happen. Your boss probably expects you to pick up the pieces and put them together in a better fashion. Or to come up with a new and better idea. Or to have the courage to stand up for what you believe in and to justify your idea. When you're dealing with businessmen, don't take things personally.

However, some things happen in business that are very personal. Many years ago I worked for a man who not only had a combative nature but also used sexual harassment as his weapon of choice. It became obvious to me that he wanted to see another woman who worked with the company take over my job. To fire me was not an option, because I worked hard and gave him no ammunition to launch an unwarranted attack. So he took another tack. He began humiliating me at every turn, sometimes in front of others, but most of the time in private.

The attacks were subtle at first, so much so that I thought the problem was me, not him. But soon the veil lifted from my eyes and I was able to see the harassment for what it really was. His crowning moment came before a group of local dignitaries who were visiting our workplace. I was charged with helping to meet and greet these people of influence and stature. During a quiet moment, my troublesome supervisor separated himself from the group and came over to make small talk with me. I decided this would be a good time to tell him about a troublesome piece of newly installed machinery we were standing next to. I explained how a lever had been attached incorrectly and described how, in order to make it operate, I had to get down on my hands and knees underneath the desk and extend my arms as far as they could reach. I asked if he could please send an engineer to fix it so I could reach it more readily.

He gave me his answer with a smirk on his face, in a voice loud enough for every impressive person in the room to hear. "I don't know why you have a problem with it. Being on your hands and knees should be a normal position for you." His reference, of course, was sexual. There was no mistaking his meaning; his leer gave him away. It was obvious to me he wanted others to believe there was some sort of sexual intimacy between us, which there never was. I flushed with embarrassment as I looked around the room to see who had heard the harsh comment.

I had enough witnesses that day to file a lawsuit, but I decided instead to give him exactly what I believed he wanted: my quitting. However, I did it on my terms and not his. I sent out résumés, went on interviews, and found a new, better-paying job within six months. I didn't like ugly confrontations, and, at that time in my life, I truly believed this was the better way of handling the situation. In retrospect, I question my decision not to report him to higher management. To this day, I'm left wondering if he's harassing other women and if my reporting him could have kept that from happening.

## THINGS WOMEN SAY THAT MAKE MEN CRAZY

Putting the shoe on the other foot, there's one thing some women do that absolutely drives a man right up the wall. It's saying, "I'm sorry," over and over again, ad nauseam. It's like playing tennis with a beginner who apologizes every time she hits the ball out, which is every time. It's bad enough you can't get the ball in play, but the situation is made worse by those endless "I'm sorries."

What are we so sorry about? Why do we say it even when we don't mean it? Why do we feel we have to apologize all the time? Those two simple words when uttered by a woman have a different ring in men's ears. Often, women mean "I'm sorry" as a gesture of sympathy. Men take it as an apology or a sign of weakness.

# COMMUNICATING WITH A DIFFICULT PERSON

I know very few people who enjoy confrontation, but standing tall in a war of words seems, unfortunately, to be a necessary part of life. It's never easy to communicate with a difficult person, but we can accomplish this feat with a minimum of frustration by following a few simple steps.

First, never shy away from a confrontation, no matter how frightened or upset you are. When someone's giving you a rough time, use all that pent-up anger or fear inside you positively. Make eye contact. Stay in control. Effective communication is a skill, not an emotion. So try not to be swept away on a tide of fear and hurt feelings. Ground yourself by not panicking and not ever taking the situation personally. Remember, it's the other person who has the problem, not you.

Keep as calm as possible. Think rationally how to solve the problem and what the best method is for presenting your solution. Then go ahead and do so with confidence and strength. Don't be personally affected by anything negative the other person has to say. Detach your emotions and keep calm, and chances are good you will come up with a workable solution and reach mutual understanding—even if you fail to reach mutual agreement.

The only time this method doesn't work is when you come up against a bully. If you get into a battle with a bully, don't expect to win. You never will. Even if you're right, the bully will find a way to turn it around to his benefit. Bullies enjoy the battle. They never lose; that's why they're bullies.

There is only one way to handle this kind of trouble. Communicate in your firmest voice, "I know this is important. I know we should talk about this, but not now, and not like this." Be firm. Make your point. Then walk away. There is no shame in backing off from this kind of hostile confrontation.

## PULL OUT THE STOPS TO GET WHAT YOU WANT

I summoned forth all my best communication techniques the first time I met and interviewed Dan Quayle. Quayle was making a campaign stop in Dayton, Ohio, during his 1988 run for the White House. I arranged the interview and then did my homework. I gathered all the information I could about this man who would be "a heartbeat away from the presidency." What I found out disheartened me, because to do my job properly I would have to ask Quayle the most insulting questions.

He was fodder for a seemingly angry press, which he had challenged early on in his candidacy. That proved to be a huge miscalculation on his part. The media spared him no mercy as they dissected his every step and misstep in the daily papers and on the nightly television news. Throughout his candidacy, Quayle was lampooned and ridiculed regularly by almost every comic in America. Talk began to surface. The public, the pollsters, and the so-called spin doctors all wondered if this Kennedyesque-appearing candidate was an asset or a liability to the election of George Bush.

Oh great, here I was about to sit down with one of the most powerful men in our country, and I would have to ask him the questions he didn't want to answer: "How does it feel to be considered a buffoon and a joke by much of America?" and "Are you hurting Bush's run for the White House? Should you step aside?"

Moreover, I had to ask these questions in a way that would ensure my success. I needed to get him to answer to the best of his ability and not just brush me off—or worse yet, walk out of the interview and leave me talking to an empty chair. That is when I fell back on my strong communication techniques.

I know I have to establish rapport in some way with the person I'm interviewing. It could be something such as helping him to his chair or getting him a drink of water—which in this case was forbidden by the Secret Service, who tested his water before he sipped.

Knowing the confrontation that lay ahead, I began to feel apprehensive. My self-confidence began to drop until I reminded myself that I was a talented and successful reporter who possessed the necessary skills to get the job done.

I took a deep breath and strode confidently over to the would-be vice president. I sported a dazzling smile. I proffered my hand first, reaching out to give him a good, hearty handshake, one that communicated strength rather than insecurity. I took the lead in all matters, welcomed him, and invited him to sit down. I made like a good hostess even though I was in a back area of a convention hall and was a guest there myself. I took control of the situation and laid out the rules. I found several positive things to compliment him about and slowly moved my chair a little closer to establish a feeling of warmth and closeness—a tough thing to do when you're surrounded by an army of Secret Service men and women. As I communicated warmth and friendliness, I felt Quayle's guard begin to relax a bit.

I began asking him all the puff questions—those he would enjoy answering, because he would get the opportunity to talk about his successes rather than his failures. More intimacy and good feelings were established. A good reporter always asks the bulk of her questions before getting to the rough stuff. That way, if the subject walks out or refuses to answer the tough questions, at least she has something to show for the effort.

Then I hit him with the unsettling questions that most Americans wanted answers to, particularly how he felt about his every misstep becoming fodder for the comedians and an unfriendly media, which seemingly took joy in heralding his latest miscue.

Quayle was not amused. His countenance changed from a pleasant expression to one of serious concern. I froze briefly as I waited for his next move, but I didn't blink. He thought for a moment and then answered my questions. He actually looked stunned and disappointed. I think he expected that kind of tough treatment from the national media but was surprised to find this kind of questioning in Dayton, Ohio, the heartland where everyone is supposed to be kind and friendly.

But because we had reached a mutual understanding, even though he didn't like where I was coming from, he understood and received the message I was sending—that of a no-nonsense reporter who was ripping through the campaign rhetoric to ask the questions my viewers most wanted him to answer.

Six years later, after the loss of the 1992 election to the Clinton-Gore ticket, I talked to Quayle again. With the stress of campaigning long gone and the addition of a few gray hairs, his manner had changed markedly, which, of course, altered the way I handled the interview. This time he approached me on a less adversarial level. He was friendly, relaxed, and warm. As a result, there was less confrontation and more fact-finding on my part. Unlike the first time around, this was a pleasant experience.

# A FINAL NOTE ON COMMUNICATION

Understanding personality types—ours and others—makes communication easier. Once we're able to determine our particular social styles, we find it so much easier to communicate with others. And once we better understand who we are and how we transmit our messages, we can more easily figure out the most effective way to communicate with people who have different styles.

To this end, I designed a special personality profile test. It helps a woman identify her own style, then offers instructions on how to successfully communicate with people who are different. If you'd like more information about the personality profile, write or call me. My address is listed at the end of this book.

# CHAPTER 9

---

# STEP SEVEN:
# FOCUS YOUR VISION

*"I think the key is for women not to set any limits."*

—Martina Navratilova

O nce upon a time, there was a young girl who wanted nothing more than to walk and run with other children, but polio paralyzed her left leg. She moved slowly and awkwardly. It was difficult enough for her to walk, much less run.

Like the fictional hero of Hollywood's *Forrest Gump*, she was forced to wear a special shoe fitted with a leg brace until she was nine years old. Nonetheless, neither she nor her mother ever lost hope that someday she would be one of the fastest women runners in the world. You see, they shared a vision of her not only as a child racing around the playground with her friends, but also as a young woman proudly sporting a chestful of Olympic medals. No matter what obstacles they faced, mother and daughter faced them together. They never took their eyes from the prize, their shared vision of Olympic Gold.

Even though it sounds like a fairy tale, this is the real-life adventure of renowned athlete Wilma Rudolph. It's the story that best illustrates the power of having a vision for one's life.

Wilma, an African-American, was one of twenty-two children. Through the years, she and her mom did whatever it took to turn their vision into reality, and that often meant a great deal of sacrifice. The first effort was to strengthen Wilma's weak limb so she could run and jump with her friends.

"My mother was the one who made me work, made me believe that one day it would be possible for me to walk without braces," said Wilma as she recalled with pride the day she was finally able to shed her cumbersome supports. Once Wilma started running, she never looked back. She quickly surpassed her peers, not only overcoming her physical challenge but also going on to excel in basketball and track. Her dedication proved outstanding as she raced toward the realization of her dream, her vision of becoming a world- class athlete.

The mother–daughter pair's investment of time, energy, faith, and hope finally paid off when Wilma was twenty. At the 1960 Olympic games in Rome, she brought the crowd to their feet as she became the first woman in history to win three gold medals in track and field. Later, her Olympian vision expanded to encompass young, future hopefuls whom she helped train. She became a coach who led by example. The story of Wilma Rudolph serves as an inspiring example of how much we can accomplish when we have a clear and focused vision.

# LOOK TO THE FUTURE

The power of vision is incredible. Once we start looking to our future—at what we can become—instead of dwelling on our past or moaning about our present, we reach things that until then far exceeded our grasp.

People who lack vision wander aimlessly through life. Occasionally they get lucky and manage to accomplish positive things, but those small achievements don't come close to the greatness they could have achieved if they'd possessed a clear and focused vision of what they wanted to become and how they wanted to live in their future— and if they'd possessed the passion to make it happen.

A vision is more than a mental picture. It's an inspiring feeling that connects every fiber of our bodies. Once we see it clearly and feel it's right for us, our vision ignites our emotion and stimulates our passion. Like the sugarplums that dance in a young child's head at Christmas, visions for ourselves and our futures form in all of us as we start life. How many times as children were we asked, "What do you want to be when you grow up?" Many of us knew with certainty. Even at a young age we possessed a vision of what we wanted to become—a dream as fragile as a soap bubble dancing in the sunlight. But too many of us lost sight of our vision as we grew older. Affected by all the negative conditioning that surrounded us, our vision became so blurred and distorted it popped and vanished.

Negative conditioning snips the tenuous connection we have to our vision. In the eagerness of youth, we become so excited about our vision that we start sharing it with anyone who will listen. But others, who can't see it, either don't believe in it or feel threatened by it. They say, "You can't do that!" or "What do you mean you want to be a doctor?

Nobody in our family is smart enough—certainly not you!" Or the ever-popular, "Why would you want to do that? That's stupid!" On hearing such negative remarks, we lose our emotional-inspirational link to our vision.

This is why the story of Wilma Rudolph serves as an important example. Wilma and her mother wouldn't allow anyone or anything to sever the connection they had to their shared vision of Wilma as an Olympic athlete. They passionately protected their dream and kept stoking the emotional fires to continually heighten the flames of their desire, thereby keeping the passion flowing until they successfully accomplished their vision.

A strong vision puts us into the future so we don't get caught up in day-to-day problems. Continually looking at the big picture, we no longer worry about petty people or fret over what actions to take. Decisions and choices become very clear-cut when we possess vision. There is no equivocation once we know exactly where we're headed. Something will either help our vision or hurt it.

Every time we're asked to make a choice or decision, we should compare it to our vision. If it fits in, we move ahead with confidence. If not, we forget it. We no longer waste precious time vacillating, fluctuating, or equivocating. Our vision sets us free and gives us the encouragement to become the best we can be.

## ENVISIONING YOUR FUTURE

Long before I ever wanted to become a television reporter and anchor, I had a very different vision of what my future would be like. It was a vision that burned deeply inside of me. As a little girl, I would sit in front of the television screen and watch the parade of beauties vie for the Miss America crown every September. I would pretend I was one of them.

I knew with certainty that I wanted to be competing on that Miss America stage in Atlantic City when I grew up. That was my vision. I dreamt about it, talked about it, and planned for it.

Knowing that the Miss Americas of my generation were expected to be virtuous and pure, I didn't drink or smoke. My teenage girlfriends were always tempting me to imbibe, but I refused. I never told them why, because I felt they would laugh at me. They would find my vision of becoming Miss America foolish. Actually, it sounded pretty silly to me. Who was I to think so much of myself? But my emotions ignited my passion. I saw my vision clearly, and it felt right for me.

I learned how to dance so I would have a talent for the competition, and I began working on my appearance—making the most of what I had. I entered one small-town pageant after another to fuel my desire and gain experience and knowledge. In rapid succession in the 1960s I became the Harvest Festival Queen, the Cranberry Festival Queen, and Miss Bristol County, and then, in 1968, I finally won the title of Miss Wareham, a Miss America preliminary pageant. I slept with my crown on the nightstand and my dreams close to my heart. I knew without a doubt I had what it took to be Miss Wareham. But here's where my vision began to falter. Now that I had made it this far, I started to listen to the naysayers who didn't believe in my abilities. My inspiration turned to fear and my emotion to stress. Each hour that brought me closer to the Miss Massachusetts pageant also brought more insecurity. The negative conditioning was now detaching me from my vision.

On the first day of competition, I entered the auditorium slightly off balance. Overwhelmed by seeing more than fifty contestants who each possessed the same aspirations I did,

I began to protect myself from the pain of ultimately losing by mentally lowering my standards. "Well, if I can't be Miss Massachusetts, maybe I can win a swimsuit or talent award."

As the week swiftly drew to a close, I had failed to win a single preliminary award. Then it was time for the televised finals in which the judges separate the winners from the losers by choosing the top ten. Only those ten contestants would still have a shot at winning the crown. Like it or not, all of us were expected to be on the stage smiling for the camera when the important announcement was made. To make matters worse, this televised moment would capture the attention of everyone I knew back in my hometown—the people expecting my success and the others looking forward to my failure. Which would it be? I felt the pressure acutely.

Two days before the final event, the organizers informed us that on the final night of competition, the top ten contestants would find their talent props, swimsuits, and evening gowns moved to a special place behind the stage immediately following the announcement so they would not have to return to the large dressing room shared by all. It was another form of segregating the winners from the losers.

Just before I entered the stage for the finals, I glanced over my shoulder and happened to see one of the helpers removing my things, along with those of several others, to the segregated area. "Wonderful!" I exclaimed to myself. "I must have made it!" My heart leapt with excitement as I proudly became poised to take the next step that would bring me closer to realizing my cherished vision—that of becoming Miss America. Overjoyed, I strode out on the stage and down the runway, exuding the self-confidence that had seemed to be in short supply all week. I knew that at any moment, the mistress of ceremonies, a former Miss America, would call my name.

She began announcing the names alphabetically—city by city. As Miss Wareham, I knew I had a while to wait. Finally, only one place remained to round out the top ten. My knees were locked and shaking, my fingers crossed so tightly they had turned white. Then she leaned into the microphone and called Miss Woburn. It was over. My dream shattered into tiny pieces.

But my pain and embarrassment didn't end there. It intensified as I walked offstage, my face hot with shame, my mouth locked in a phony smile pressed tightly over my teeth. I wanted to crawl into a corner and hide, but one of the volunteers backstage called me over to the segregated area for the winners. I thought she was going to comfort me, but nothing could be further from the truth.

"Get over here and get your things out of the way. It's all over for you but we don't want you getting in the winners' way as they continue the competition."

I couldn't believe her cruelty. With shoulders hunched and spirit gone, I walked to the winners' circle to pick up my wardrobe, tears pricking and stinging my eyes. Awkwardly I carted my personal items back to the room with the thirty-nine other losers—all of whom were exhibiting various states of distress. It seems I had been number eleven, and they had moved my stuff to the winner's circle just in case one of the ten women who'd been chosen to perform their talents on television collapsed or became injured. In other words, I was the designated back-up.

Instead of being pleased to have come that close, I felt destroyed. I had worked my heart out, giving it all I had, only to find out it wasn't enough. I felt I would never again be able to show my face in Wareham. I had let the entire town down, but, more important, I had failed, and my vision of parading to Atlantic City as a winner was demolished beyond repair. The week was one of the most painful of my life.

Looking back, with all the emotion removed from the picture, I realize my vision then wasn't strong enough for me to succeed. Had it really been the right vision for me, I would have refused to accept that failure as an option. Instead, I would have used it as a learning experience and tried again.

Today, I have my vision and believe in it wholeheartedly. I am resolved to be successful and prepared to protect my vision. What other people think or feel about it has no effect on me. Nothing can separate me from what I want to become.

As bad as it was, however, my Miss America "debacle" did produce something wonderful. As a result of holding on to that vision for so many of my growing up years and wanting to be good enough to win, I had kept away from the drugs and alcohol that brought down so many of my teenaged counterparts. During those years, I worked to keep my mind alert and my body healthy. I learned a great deal about discipline and desire.

Although I didn't become Miss America, all that training became good preparation for being a public figure. Much of what I learned in my pageant days helps me handle my life today as a television anchor. So, although my teenaged vision did not lead to the path I thought it should at the time, it did me a world of good.

## CREATE A POWERFUL VISION

Think of all the energy we expend each day doing a myriad of different things. Each one seems important at the time, but after adding them all up, we often find they are unrelated to helping us become the person we want to be in the future.

Vision is like having a movie director calling all the shots in our life, pulling together all the pieces of our life in the same way that she pulls together all the scenes of a successful film. Vision always looks at the big picture, providing a long-range focus to direct our energies so we stop wasting time on nonproductive activities.

Creating our vision requires a great deal of soul-searching and thought. We can no longer go with the flow, let nature take its course, or choose the path of least resistance. Once we decide who we want to become, what we want to be, and where we want to go, our lives take on direction and meaning. Once we put our hand to the tiller and chart our own course, we are no longer the rudderless ship that keeps getting swept away with the outgoing tide of other people's wants, desires, and needs.

A good, clear, and focused vision will steer your ship out of the choppy waters churned up by other people's agendas and into a safe harbor where you control your own destiny.

## MAKE YOURSELF A TOP PRIORITY

Establishing our vision means spending time alone with our thoughts. It means getting in touch with our feelings to form a picture of ourselves in the future. We need to isolate ourselves from others to be free of their influence.

Your vision is exactly that—your vision. It is not based on the wishes of your parents, children, spouse, friends, or coworkers. Creating a vision to please other people never works, mostly because there's no emotion to inspire you.

# FINDING YOUR VISION

## WHAT DO YOU WANT TO ACHIEVE IN THE SEVEN AREAS OF YOUR LIFE?

FAMILY

CAREER

FINANCIAL

SOCIAL

PHYSICAL

MENTAL

SPIRITUAL

# DEFINING YOUR VISION

Coming up with a clear vision of where you see yourself in the future sounds like an almost impossible task, but there's an easy way to make it manageable. Please look at the worksheet on the opposite page.

1. Take as much time as you need to examine all the choices life has to offer you for each of the seven areas in your life.
2. For each, describe the picture of yourself you see in your future. Don't do just what's safe. Try taking some chances. Resist falling back into your comfort zone.
3. Keep in mind: your vision is exactly that—your vision. It is determined by you, not by others. Don't create your vision to please others. That never works.
4. Don't create a false vision. Be true to yourself.
5. Base your vision on strong principles, morals, and beliefs, or it will not survive.

You do need to use your imagination for this exercise. Think not of what you are today; think of what you have the power to become in each of the seven areas of your life. Consider all seven, or your vision will be limited.

Mary Kay Ash, the cosmetics queen famous for awarding pink Cadillacs to deserving saleswomen, offers this wonderful observation about reaching your vision. "Aerodynamically the bumble bee shouldn't be able to fly, but the bumble bee doesn't know it, so it goes on flying anyway." Ash is saying that the only limits to your vision are the ones you set yourself.

For years, I operated with limited vision. My only concern was my career, and I sacrificed everything for it. I set aggressive goals when it came to being a television journalist, but I had no time for anything else. The first thing I sacrificed was a family. I felt I couldn't successfully handle a career and children both, so I put all my energies into my work and put the family on hold.

The next thing I lost were my friends. As a young up-and-coming TV anchor, I was working all the time, even weekends. For a while my friends called, asking me to join them in skiing or just meeting for a drink after work. But I was too busy. They soon stopped calling. My seven-day-a-week workdays often sapped my physical strength. I never worked out at the gym, never had time.

Then I began to lose my faith. As I became overwhelmed at work, I lost touch with the higher power in my life. On the job, my stories began to lack the punch they previously had, as I became too mentally tired to do the research necessary to make them award winners. By neglecting six of the seven areas of my life, I was sacrificing my future and the respect and esteem that my superiors had formerly held for me.

I became physically drained and emotionally barren. I went home every night to an empty house. I lacked the company of friends and family. My days were filled with activity; my nights ached with loneliness. I had reached my skewed vision, but at what price? My vision was poorly thought-out and severely limited to only one of the seven areas in my life.

At this point, I began to do a lot of soul-searching, taking time alone and examining all seven areas of my life. I built a new picture of me based on all the pieces of my life, not just my career, and I reworked my vision to the point of understanding my true identity.

## IDENTITY VERSUS ROLE

Many of us wear many different hats: mother, daughter, wife, friend, employer, employee, doctor, nurse, secretary,

# How Many Balls Can You Juggle Before Dropping Them?

supervisor, and so on. These are the roles we play in life, which are usually determined by our primary areas of responsibility.

Unfortunately, many of us confuse our roles with our identity. We seem to lose ourselves by either being pushed into a role because it's how other people see us, or being forced into a role by circumstances. The danger comes when we get so caught up in our roles that we lose our true identity.

Our identity differs from the roles we play. Our identity is our inner being, made up of the many characteristics we possess.

Think about it this way. If you're stripped naked, standing out in the middle of an expansive open field, who are you? There are no children around, so you can't be a mother. No husband, so you can't be a wife. You're certainly not a fashion model because you don't have any clothes. So look inward.

As you stand there, naked and isolated from the rest of society, what remains is totally on the inside—those qualities and characteristics that make you the person you are—in other words, your inner being. Here are your feelings, emotions, love, kindness, competence, self-assurance, strength, and that indescribable essence that singles you out from other human beings. Without all the trappings from the various roles we play, what remains is our true identity.

As we move into our different roles—mother, wife, sister, lover, worker, business owner, and so on—we need to make sure we don't lose our true identity. Those special characteristics that make up our inner being must be transmitted to the many roles we play in life.

Usually, I see myself as a kind, loving, and extremely

understanding person who likes and enjoys other people, but whenever I bump into someone I just can't tolerate, I seem to slip into an alter ego. I become guarded and suspicious, a role that is definitely not me. Instead of being my usually open and garrulous self, which is the core of my inner being, I start talking in short, clipped sentences, asking few questions and volunteering little information. The expansive smile that always comes readily to my lips appears frozen and wooden instead.

Although the behavior of others often constrains us to act in certain ways, what we really should be doing is remaining consistent and true to our own identity. Thus, I should be more tolerant and understanding when meeting someone whose company offends me. I should never allow people to push me into a role that conflicts with my identity.

When I was caught up in an abusive relationship, all I could see was how "he" was changing over the years as things grew worse. In reality, he didn't change at all. I did. At the end, he was just as he had been in the beginning, never straying far from his true identity. Had I looked carefully at all the clues while we were dating, I would have seen that his actions were very consistent. But denying reality, I forged ahead with blinders on, convinced I could make this relationship work.

Only after our relationship fell apart did I realize how far I had deviated from my true identity. As I relaxed and became less guarded, family and friends began greeting me with a chorus of, "I'm glad you're back," and they weren't talking about my proximity. What they meant was that I was acting like the Donna of old, the one who was kind, loving, and fun. Not the protective and fearful Donna who got lost in the role she was playing, that of a victim.

Conversely, maintaining my true identity while operating in my role as a TV anchor has been a major part of my success in broadcasting. I'm the same person whether on screen or off, able to successfully transmit my identity as a sincere and caring person into my role as anchor.

It's enjoyable to play many roles in life, but don't ever let the roles play you. Understanding our true identity is key to building a strong vision. We need to know exactly who we are before we can decide where we're headed.

## A STORY OF FAITH

To look at her, you would think former NBC star Faith Daniels always had a vision of becoming a successful TV anchor/reporter and the host of a nationally televised talk show. Her delicate grace makes a tough job look easy. Beautiful, charming, intelligent, and clever, Faith is a woman whose rise to the big time was steady and sure. To know Faith is to love her; she is one of the most good-humored and unaffected celebrities I know.

I remember talking with her in the make-up room of the Pittsburgh TV station where we both worked as reporters. It was 1984 and she had yet to land her big network job. She looked gorgeous that day. I teased her because it was obvious she had something up her sleeve.

She told me she was flying to Texas after the six o'clock news to interview for an anchor job at a major station. She said she wasn't too keen about going; it was her agent's idea. Apparently they didn't share the same vision. Her agent wanted her to ace a big job with a big salary—of which he would get a percentage, of course—but Faith cared more about family.

Having been adopted by a loving couple in a small city near Pittsburgh, Faith always cared about family more than fame. She was content with the job she held, a job that had brought her back home after stints in Illinois and West Virginia. She had a wonderful husband, Dean—a television producer who supported her and loved her, and still does. They were planning to have children.

Still, fame beckoned. The job in Texas didn't work out, but on the heels of that came a remarkable offer. CBS wanted Faith to anchor the news on its national morning show. The bright lights of the Big Apple called, but Faith resisted the lure. She turned it down. The network sweetened the pot, and Faith turned it down again.

But the third time proved irresistible, and Faith was swept up to CBS. Her husband, a great talent in his own right, also found work in New York at a local television station.

It was at CBS that Faith made a name for herself before pushing on to NBC, anchoring news, reporting, and ultimately hosting a national talk show bearing her name. By the time the show *Dateline* summoned her services as a correspondent in 1993, Faith had three children. She had taken a good hard look at her career and her vision, and she had found her life greatly out of balance.

The *Dateline* job would require months of traveling each year. Her husband's job required him to travel as well. Sometimes their travels were expected to occur at the same time, but always, it seemed, in different directions. Faith says NBC offered her a reduced travel schedule of no more than ten days a month to try to keep her on staff, but in the end she had to decline.

Faith's vision was always family first, career second; and she always understood her true identity apart from the role she played on television. She forged ahead with her demanding career as long as it didn't negatively affect her family. When it began to, Faith says she made the call to be a full-time mother to her three children. She has no regrets. Faith Daniels never lost sight of her number one priority.

## BALANCING YOUR LIFE

In developing your own vision, a key factor is to strive for a balanced life. Think about the seven areas of your life as seven balls you must constantly juggle. Each ball represents an area of importance: family, career, financial, social, physical, mental, and spiritual. All of them are important to developing yourself as a whole person, but three of them are of primary importance: physical, mental, and spiritual. If you are not mentally tough, spiritually strong, and physically fit, you'll drop the balls in the secondary areas of your life: family, career, financial, and social.

When we make our choices based *solely* on family, financial, career, and social needs, we ignore the primary areas. Without concentrating on our mental, spiritual, and physical well-being, we run out of gas, falling short of our destination.

Take a look at the woman on page 187. She's really sweating it out trying to juggle all seven balls. It won't be long before she drops more of them. Is that a picture of you? Are you working desperately to keep all those balls in the air? Which ones are you dropping?

Chances are you're sacrificing your primary areas as you labor to take care of your family, job, finances, and friends. But that's a huge mistake. Covering the three primary areas energizes us, thus enhancing our secondary areas.

Let's say, for example, that something's going wrong at work. You're working hard but not getting anywhere. So you work even harder, putting more effort into the job. You're like a loaded train chugging up a steep incline. "I

# YOU STOP DROPPING THE BALL WHEN EVERYTHING CENTERS ON YOUR OWN SPIRITUAL, MENTAL AND PHYSICAL NEEDS

know I can, I know I can!" you say as you chug along, but your wheels are slipping and you're sliding back down the hill. Nothing, it seems, can stop the skid.

You keep pushing until you can't push any more. This is the time to dig deep into your reserve to pull out more energy, but you find there's nothing left. In your rush to the top, you neglected the primaries: the mental, spiritual, and physical areas of your life. Taking care of the primaries keeps us healthy, strong, and better equipped to handle life's problems.

The drawing on page 193 illustrates the difference. Here's a calm, cool, and collected woman who has her house, her job, and her life in order. She is able to successfully balance the balls representing her career, family, social, and financial spheres because she relies on a strong foundation of mental, physical, and spiritual health.

## HERE'S THE PLAN

Your vision, identity, and the three primary areas of your life—physical, mental, and spiritual—all force you to look inward and see the long-range picture. If we build our vision on the roles we play rather than on our true identity, we become unhappy. Take the example of the mother who establishes her vision around her children to the exclusion of everything else. When they leave home, she loses her identity. She feels unfulfilled and unsatisfied.

Or consider the career woman who builds her vision around her profession. It seems satisfying in the beginning when she's on the fast track to success. But that picture changes drastically when the company falls on hard times and is forced to let her go.

It happened to me when my young dream of becoming Miss America failed to materialize. I fell apart.

# $M$Y VISION

_____

_____

_____

_____

_____

_____

_____

_____

_____

_____

_____

_____

Instead of letting such limited visions keep *you* off balance, probe your innermost feelings and make your vision a true picture of satisfaction, contentment, and happiness.

Look intently at the seven areas of your life. Then turn to the worksheet on page 195. In one or two paragraphs, take all the information gleaned from your introspection and write a description of yourself in the future. Remember to be true to your identity rather than to your roles.

Our vision is one of the most precious gifts we can give ourselves, but it survives only if we build it on a foundation of truth. Anything else, and we're cheating ourselves. If our vision is based on a lie or an illusion, it will crumble, like the shanty on the beach that is exposed to the everyday pounding of the surf. We are then left feeling discouraged and cynical.

## TAKE YOUR PASSION AND MAKE IT HAPPEN

Establishing a vision that is truly ours requires a leap of faith. We need to believe, without a doubt, that the picture we paint today of our future selves will one day become a completed portrait of our lives.

Whenever life provides us with an awkward moment, we must focus clearly on our vision and not lose sight of it, making our vision so ingrained in our inner being that it becomes the most compelling force behind every decision we make.

Obstacles fall by the wayside as we move forward toward our vision with passion and enthusiasm. Like Olympic medalist Wilma Rudolph, we must keep our eyes on the prize. With hard work, we can shed our mental and emotional handicaps as she shed her braces.

# CHAPTER 10

# STEP EIGHT: GOALS WILL GET YOU THERE

*"A good goal is like a strenuous exercise—it makes you stretch."*

—*Mary Kay Ash*

I'm going to go to the big city and become a star!" Those are the prophetic words printed in the high school year book of one of my neighbors back in the tiny hamlet of Wareham, Massachusetts, a place known as the "Gateway to Cape Cod."

Even in her tender teen years, this would-be actress knew more about having goals than I ever did. Each time I view one of her movies today, I am awed by the fact that she achieved her biggest goals in life and did so with spectacular results. She adopted a single-minded purpose early in life, and she pursued it with passion.

In high school this gal stood head and shoulders above her classmates. Today, many of her leading men still have to look up to her. She has a slight overbite, which in her school days was considered unfortunate. But today it's one of her most alluring features.

A small-town girl, she wanted to go to Hollywood and become one of the brightest stars to shine in the Tinseltown firmament. To reach that long-term goal, she set a number of smaller ones.

First, she traveled to New York City and became a model while taking acting lessons. There are hundreds of modeling agencies in New York, listed from A to Z. She applied to each one in alphabetical order.

Doors slammed and opportunities vanished at one agency after another, but still she remained confident about completing her goals. Finally, she reached the Zoli agency, which accepted her.

Her never-say-die attitude paid off when film director Sydney Pollack spotted her in the Victoria's Secret catalog modeling lingerie. He immediately cast her in a small role in his next film—a movie blockbuster that catapulted her into the public's line of vision, and what a vision she was. Picture this: she's in a dressing room with only a bra and panties on, sporting an amazingly flat stomach, and in walks the "woman" she's sharing the room with, only he's a man dressed as a woman, Dustin Hoffman. Her role in the movie *Tootsie* gave her a measure of success, but she was still far from a major Hollywood player.

The next time I saw her was on television in a Dabney Coleman series called *Buffalo Bill*. I thought, "No one-shot wonder, she's on her way!"

Sometime after that she won a guest spot on *Family Ties*, playing Michael J. Fox's older love interest. She towered over him majestically, and he looked up in awe at her sexy little overbite.

Then she made a series of successful films, her long-term goal of Hollywood superstardom moving into the range of her sights: *The Fly, Earth Girls Are Easy,* and *Beetle Juice.*

These triumphs were followed by her greatest achievement to date. She had read the book *The Accidental Tourist,* and she knew with certainty she could play the part of the kooky dog trainer for all it's worth. She fought vigorously for the right to play the role of Muriel, and upon getting it, she let out all the stops. She won an Oscar for that performance.

Academy Award winner and Wareham High School graduate Geena Davis set a goal and never deviated from achieving it, despite what anyone else said or did. No matter what trials she faced, Geena always believed that success was "just around the corner."

Today, Geena has not only realized a substantial portion of her vision, that of becoming a full-fledged star of the first magnitude, but also expanded her vision through the years to encompass many things not included in her original picture of success. She has become a movie producer with clout who works to provide opportunities for others in addition to herself.

No empty-headed starlet, Geena is a talented woman who knows what she's got and understands exactly what to do with it. She chooses her roles carefully and never fears breaking through barriers to change the world's perception of women. There were those who believed a women's "buddy" movie would never take off. They ate their words when *Thelma and Louise* made movie history in 1991.

There's a world full of talented people out there who will never even come close to reaching the heights Geena has. They have loads of ability but accomplish absolutely nothing because they don't understand the importance of having goals. They lack direction and the ability to use goal-setting to get what they want.

No matter how much knowledge and ability we possess, we will experience only minimal success if we don't set goals. Accomplishing her goals is what sets Geena Davis apart from the thousands of hopefuls who arrive in Hollywood each year.

## BECOME A CONTINUAL GOAL-SETTER

Think of goal-setting as your personal ladder to success. Picture a house. See the roof? That's your vision. You reach that vision only by placing a ladder against the side of the house and taking each step one by one. Each rung you climb is the completion of a goal you've set for yourself. You keep climbing until you reach the roof—your vision.

Unlike your vision, which answers the question, "What do you want to become," goals answer the question, "What do you want to have." In other words, if you want to become something, you have a vision. If you want to have something, that's a goal. A vision is a long-term inspirational picture of yourself that's charged with emotion. Goals are more pragmatic. Goals are the deliberate steps we take to successfully become what we want most to be.

At first, conjuring up a real-life example of goal-setting from my own personal files had me stumped. I wracked my brain, searching for the best way to illustrate this point, but I failed to come up with one time in my past when I'd sat down and actually laid out a written plan of long- and short-range goals to complete so I could reach my vision—that of becoming a successful and independent person with enough power and influence to help others, to become the best that I could be.

After drawing a blank for days, I gave up and called Mom. She chuckled as she heard my latest dilemma. "Donna, think about it. You've been setting goals your whole life. Sure, you didn't write them down but that doesn't mean you weren't doing it subconsciously." Mom was right.

Many of us establish a vision and set goals for ourselves without ever realizing it. It's something we do automatically, like breathing. My vision has always been to be the best I can be and to be successful. Therefore, I had set goals to be successful in everything I did.

When I was a Brownie Scout at the tender age of six, my goal was to accomplish each task to the best of my ability so I could be successful. As I grew into a Girl Scout, I earned every badge possible in the time allotted and wouldn't stop until I was awarded the Curved Bar, which is a great honor in Girl Scouting. It symbolizes success in meeting every goal, doing everything asked of you and more.

After Girl Scouts came Rainbow Girls. I was in junior high school then and wanted more than anything to be a Rainbow Girl, an offshoot of the Masons and Eastern Star organizations. I saw myself wearing beautiful white dresses and gowns and becoming proficient at memorizing pages and pages of ritual—words of wisdom to deliver to the other young ladies at the appropriate time.

Shortly after becoming part of the organization, I decided that to realize my vision meant working my way up through every color of the rainbow to the exalted position of Worthy Advisor—a journey that would take almost five years. Carefully and strategically, I planned out my ascension to the top tier of the organization. Each goal mapped out and completed, I became Worthy Advisor in my senior year in high school. After a year in that lofty position, I was awarded the highest honor—the Grand Cross of Colors—for outstanding service.

With that success tucked securely under my belt, I moved on. Next stop was the pageant circuit to fulfill my great desire of becoming Miss America. But, as you have seen, that poorly enacted vision became derailed. I did not become Miss America or even Miss Massachusetts. Having gotten used to working hard and winning, I experienced my first major defeat at the state finals. However, the experience reinforced the importance of goal-setting. I learned that we can't do a thing halfway. We need to continually set goals. When the grueling competition for Miss Massachusetts became almost unbearable, I let myself down because I failed to continue setting goals to reach the top. I lost sight of my vision—to be the best I could be—and the specific steps I needed to take to get there.

After licking my wounds a while, I was soon ready to start moving forward again. I took my energies and devoted them entirely to finding a successful career. I started out as a telephone operator and worked my way into an entry-level management position with the New England Telephone Company. Realizing that was not for me, I moved on and tried something else. For several years, nothing seemed to fit. None of the jobs I held offered me the kind of success I was searching for—until I found my secretarial job at the television station. I knew with certainty, at that moment, television would be my chosen career field. Being a television journalist would definitely make me a success and could ultimately bring me the power that would allow me to influence others—which, of course, was my true vision for myself.

There was no stopping me once I stepped through the door. I selected comic book heroine Lois Lane as my mentor. Before you laugh, consider this. Lois Lane is adventurous, strong, confident, successful, kind, capable, skilled journalistically, and hard-working, and she dates Superman. What more could a woman want?

I set my sights high on a television anchor position and wouldn't stop until I reached it. It wasn't an easy climb to the top, but this time, unlike what I had seen happen to my vision of becoming Miss America, I would not become detached from my inspiration. Becoming a television anchor was the right choice for me—a vision that would never lose focus. It offered me everything my heart desired—success, independence, and influence to help others.

Mentally, I made up a long-range plan of how to achieve my vision, and I never deviated from it. I set a series of long- and short-range goals and completed each one of them in its own time. First, I won a job as a radio reporter in 1975, then went back to school to become more educated. In 1976, I moved into television, hosting daily one-minute community bulletins and monthly half-hour public affairs shows. Within six months, I made my move to TV reporter. I worked longer hours than any of the others, took writing and elocution classes, accepted the assignments others refused as beneath them, and learned about television from the bottom up. I also read voraciously—everything from periodicals to the classics. When I was asked to produce and anchor the weekend news shows a year later, I was more than equal to the challenge.

I completed my next goal when I won a position as weekday anchor/producer at a television station in Scranton, Pennsylvania. The year was 1978. It was then that I had a revelation about my future. An honest assessment of my abilities acquired thus far revealed that while I was long on anchor potential, my writing and storytelling skills were severely lacking. If I wanted to be more than window dressing on the news set, it was time to learn to become a better journalist. With that uppermost in my mind, I selected for my next goal moving out of news and into the entertainment field as co-host of *PM Magazine* in Milwaukee, Wisconsin, in the fall of 1979. In that role I would be forced to meet stringent deadlines to produce several complex and lengthy stories weekly under great pressure.

After a few false starts and failures as a story producer, I finally became adept at it. Once I accomplished that mission, it was time for me to move back into news.

So in 1982 I took a job as an investigative consumer reporter in Pittsburgh, Pennsylvania, to earn back my news stripes. At that time in the TV industry, it was frowned upon to jump from news to entertainment and back again. The powers-that-be believed one would lose credibility with the audience, and thereby be unsuccessful in communicating hard news. But once again, I set my goal to get back into news, and I didn't deviate from it. No matter what anyone said, I felt then—and still feel—that my *PM* storytelling experience was important to my growth as a strong reporter. After two years of breaking stories on the news beat in Pittsburgh, I hopped back into the anchor seat, moving to Dayton, Ohio, where I've stayed and become very successful.

If we don't set goals, life doesn't have as much meaning as it could have. When we have a purpose in life and know where we are going and how to get there, we experience joy and become energized. The biggest thrills in life come from attaining the goals we set for ourselves. Goals help us move easily from problem to solution. They inspire, motivate, and challenge us.

Goals are the signposts along the road to success. That journey begins with our vision, which we identified in the previous chapter. The next step in moving forward to realize our dreams is to map out a series of long- and short-term goals. Every time we achieve one of them and cross it off our list, we become encouraged and motivated to do more, to move forward and conquer the next one.

Each little success, every goal realized, brings us one step closer to reaching our vision.

## MAKE YOUR GOALS MEANINGFUL

We continually need to be setting meaningful goals in our lives. Some women fear doing that, saying, "What if I change my mind?" or "I prefer to leave my options open." But there's a problem with leaving our options open. We lose our focus on what's important, so we don't get much of anything accomplished.

The plan is to set realistic and doable goals for ourselves. However, just because we put them in writing doesn't mean they're set in stone. We can change our minds. Goals can be altered as the situation warrants. As our vision changes, our goals may change. Or perhaps we refine our goals as we come up with a better way to reach that vision or see another opportunity. It's good to be fluid and to adjust accordingly.

## NOT MAKING TIME TO SET GOALS IS UNACCEPTABLE

Many of us are what I like to call "taskmasters." We have our "to do" lists each day, and as we tick off the separate little tasks one by one we feel a sense of accomplishment. However, I wonder why it is that we who are so good at making lists never think to establish a vision and write down a set of goals to reach it. Think of the pride you'd feel if you were doing more than just what it takes to get through the day. We must become goal setters if we are to become and remain successful women of achievement and effective leaders.

Many women say they don't have the time to sit down and make out a list of goals, let alone follow them to completion. But they've got it backwards. Goals are time savers, not time wasters. The initial list-making investment pays off in creating *more* quality time, not less.

Others say they don't want to make goal-setting a priority because they're already overburdened and can't take on any more responsibility. What they mean is they don't want to accept responsibility for controlling their own destinies. Feeling overburdened comes from not distinguishing between one's own goals and those others set for us.

Some women feel it's easier to react to life than to set the rules. But they're wrong. Life actually gets easier and less problematic when we're in the driver's seat. Accepting responsibility for our lives and setting goals keeps us moving forward. After we achieve one goal, we set another and another. Goal-setting never stops. It is the best and easiest way to get where we want to be.

I wish I had learned this lesson earlier in life. Caught up in the present, there were times I often failed see the promise of tomorrow. Sadly, I allowed myself to get bogged down in the muck and mire of everyday life, which obscured my vision of the future.

## SETTING A "WEIGHTY" GOAL

I remember in the early seventies looking into the mirror and seeing only what I wanted to see, the slim, somewhat attractive girl who was the fortunate winner of a Miss

America preliminary pageant in 1968. But that was the young woman of several years before. In the seventies I was seeing only the image I had of myself, not the person I had become.

I stood at the full-length mirror, pulling, tugging, and willing my zipper to close. As I grunted, sweating with the effort, I finally felt it tug free. "Ommphhh," I exclaimed as the silver tag finally zipped upwards. "That wasn't so hard," I thought, my wrist aching from the effort, and then I looked down. The only reason the zipper moved freely was that it had pulled free of its stitching and was no longer part of the lifeless brown polyester pants. "What shoddy workmanship," I moaned, still not accepting what the mirror so plainly revealed.

In those days, I was not a happy woman. Whenever sad or depressed, I turned to food for comfort. Ice cream offered the best salve to soothe anxious feelings and smooth away all of life's problems. It also smoothed out more than a few wrinkles as I expanded in measure to the half-gallons of ice cream I consumed daily. Sara Lee had become my best friend. Her orange frosted cake was a favorite. I kept dozens in the freezer and popped them out as a hypochondriac pops pills from her medicine bottles. Soon, all this excess began to add up.

At 5'4", I tipped the scales at 165. At that point it became hard to deny what had happened. I was a hostess in a popular restaurant and got very tired of hearing the well-meaning clientele say, "Donna, you have such a pretty face. I bet you'd look great if you lost some weight." Suddenly, I could see myself through the eyes of others.

I looked older than my twenty-four years. My hair appeared lank and unattractive, robbed of life and vibrancy by my unhealthy diet. I had an extra chin and rolls of fat around my waist. Let's not even talk about my puffy abdomen, bulging thighs, and expansive bottom. My eyes had lost their sparkle and my heart its desire as I slowly changed from the girl I was to the woman I didn't want to be.

I was desperate to change but didn't know how to start. Instead of doing the right thing and setting realistic goals for my weight loss, I went in for every quick fix I could find, every hot new diet fad on the market that promised everything, but in the end only robbed me of my health and well-being. Looking for the easiest way out of this mess I had made of myself, I kept searching for the magic bullet that would quickly shoot away the excess pounds it had taken me years to put on.

As I yo-yoed from one method to another, I became ill and more depressed than ever. The end to this manic episode in my life finally came after I decided to fast without a doctor's supervision. In three days, I ate only half an orange while manically increasing my workout program. By the end of the fourth day, I was physically exhausted, emotionally shot, and spiritually drained. Too tired to fight back any more, I stopped to reflect on the ungodly mess I had created of my life. Once again, I turned to food for comfort to ease the pain of my dissatisfaction with myself.

For the remainder of the month, I sat around like a sad sack feeling sorry for myself, and then I got angry. My anger spurred me into action. Tired of sitting on the sidelines and watching everyone else live the life I wanted, I became motivated and determined to lose weight the healthy way by changing my attitude toward food and modifying my behavior. I began to eat a diet filled with healthful greens, oats, and pasta. I eschewed desserts for the time being, knowing that one bite of something luscious could send me spiraling off course. I set realistic and doable goals.

Acknowledging that it had taken me years to pack on the extra pounds, I had to accept the fact that successful weight loss wouldn't happen overnight. My long-range goal was to lose forty-seven pounds, but I set my short-range goals in ten-pound increments. In this way I would achieve each goal in a reasonable amount of time and not become devastated by the length of time it might take to lose all forty-seven pounds.

As I successfully met each ten-pound goal, I patted myself on the back and moved on cheerfully to meet the next goal. By the time the last seven pounds were in reach, nothing could stop me. I won't lie to you. The last seven pounds were the most difficult to lose, but by then I was so pumped up by my successful achievement of all my previous goals, I hung in until the end. Then, instead of celebrating my triumph with food, I rewarded myself with a complete makeover, a new me to go with my new attitude.

Unhealthy eating will always be a temptation for me. It's something I have to work on every day. However, I have a strong motivation to stay slim. I want to remain healthy and attractive. Being on television helps keep me honest. They say television adds ten or fifteen pounds to your appearance. So I can't afford to gain too much weight. Every day I fight the urge to go with the flow, to find comfort and solace in food. Instead, I've chosen to take charge of my life by setting good, healthful goals that lead me to a better, more successful life.

## GOOD GOALS AFFECT YOUR ENTIRE LIFE

Once you establish your vision, it's time to begin creating goals that will affect your life in the most positive of ways. Some goals fall into the urgent category and must take priority over others. Goals should address the seven important areas of life that you considered in Chapter 9: family, career, financial, social, physical, mental, and spiritual. Don't omit any one of them.

Evaluate what's really important to you. Goal-setting becomes easier when you have a clear vision and understand your true identity and values. For example, once I actually set goals and a timetable to lose weight, I felt less pressure and stress. When I went through my lazy phase in writing this book, goal-setting showed me exactly what I had to do to reach my vision of completing it. And don't forget actress Geena Davis, who never sacrifices her true identity and values as she sets goals and works toward her vision in Hollywood, a superficial place where it's easy to lose the real you and do things that don't reflect your personal values.

Goal-setting is a lifelong process that begins today. For goals to be successful, they must be very personal, honest, and realistic. Like your vision, goals are based on your needs, not on the wants and desires of other people.

If you have a vision of yourself as an entrepreneur, your goals would be made up of all the specific, pragmatic steps that will make your becoming an entrepreneur happen, such as getting educated in your field of expertise and arming yourself with the knowledge of what it takes to run a successful business. Other goals could include setting up a business plan, approaching banks for funding, renting office space, hiring workers, mapping out a strategic selling plan, and so on.

Once you've created your list of long- and short-range goals, it's important to share them with someone else. Telling them to another person helps you become committed to carrying them out. You are more likely to achieve your goals when you speak them aloud, and less likely to forgo action if you know that other people expect you to accomplish what you said you would.

Expressing goals usually works well in business. Soon after my husband and I decided to buy a small manufacturing company, we began telling people about our plans. The more people we told, the more information we accumulated about different businesses that were available to purchase. Chance meetings at dinner parties unearthed a number of venture capitalists who indicated they'd love to back a dynamic duo like my husband and me. The more people with whom we shared our goal, the more committed to it we became. In addition, as supportive people began hearing about our goal, they offered help to make our dream come true.

## A WORD TO THE WISE

When you announce your goal, it is very important to share your action plan with only those people who support your goal. People who don't share your enthusiasm or views, and those who are jealous or fearful of you, could be destructive and downright devastating. You need to form your own positive network filled with people who want only good things to happen to you.

Dieting is a perfect example. Sometimes those who are nearest and dearest to us increase our agony over our weighty problem instead of offering the help we so desperately seek. They can be patronizing, refusing to take our goal of shedding pounds seriously. "You're on *another* diet?" they say in an accusing tone, an agonizing reminder of the many times we tried before and failed.

Instead of turning to them, we can find greater support in a group of strangers who share the same challenges we face, people who have chosen to come together for the sole purpose of getting support, and who learn in the process how to give support to others.

It's not difficult to find such groups in most cities or towns. Contact a local church or synagogue, a local counseling center, therapists in private practice, a county department on aging, a hospital that runs community-based programs, and so on. All of these resources are happy to refer women to a support group that meets their particular needs.

If you aren't surrounded by positive people, think about keeping your precious goals close to your vest. Let's get back to the dieting example. After setting a goal to lose thirty pounds, you announce the plan to some of your coworkers and family members. From that day forward you become inundated by little remarks. Suddenly, your weight seems to be the hot topic, as everyone—your supportive friends as well as the nonsupportive people—keeps asking, "Have you lost any weight, yet? You don't look like you have."

Or they'll begin making comments about the food you're consuming. "Do you really think you should eat that? I know you're on a diet."

Even worse, they begin to remark about your appearance. "You're looking a little haggard, dear. Maybe you should eat something. After all, it's not good to starve yourself. One tiny piece of cake won't hurt you."

Let's face it, by being overweight you are already dealing with enough doubt, guilt, and insecurity to last two lifetimes. You don't need this kind of treatment from the people you thought liked and respected you. In a situation such as this, don't set yourself up for failure. Keep certain goals a secret, and think how wonderful it will be when others—without prompting—finally notice the new you. Once you successfully complete this goal, just think of the exhilaration you'll feel from the warmth of your supportive friends, the envy of the other kind, and your own enhanced self-esteem. The successful completion of that goal is key to reaching your vision of becoming an energetic, enthusiastic woman who is healthy and enjoys life to its fullest.

## IT'S EASY AS 1,2,3

Goals are easy to set once we know what we're doing. But to ensure success, we need to have each of our goals meet certain criteria. A goal must be honest, realistic, and designed specifically to meet our individual emotional and psychological needs, wants, and desires. Each goal must also be well thought-out and specific. Declaring that you need to lose weight this year is not a good goal. It's a broad, sweeping generalization. Rather than be vague, commit yourself to a meaningful goal of losing eight solid pounds in one month.

We must also be honest. If we don't believe we can achieve our goal, it becomes nothing more than an amusing diversion or a depressing exercise in futility. For example, it's silly for me to set a goal to become a Radio City Music Hall Rockette if I don't know how to dance, or to win a Grand Slam tennis tournament when I'm only a club-level player.

How about running a marathon? Up until now you've done little more than jog around the block, but it's a challenge you feel you need to take. If that is your goal, you have to do more than talk about it. You must take all the action steps necessary to race to the finish. You start by determining which marathon you're going to run in and how fast you want to run it. Next, you sign up for it. Then you buy the proper shoes and clothes and condition yourself by running a certain number of miles weekly. You enhance those practice runs by adding a visualization technique. As you run, visualize yourself breaking through the tape at the finish line and hearing the crowd cheer. Each one of these pragmatic steps is important to accomplishing your goal of running a marathon.

Meaningful goals work, but if yours are just vague ideas and you're not physically working toward being able to cross the finish line, it's a shallow gesture and a grave mistake. You invite failure into your life when you create meaningless goals. Each goal that goes unfulfilled makes you cynical, disillusioned, negative, and discouraged. "See, I told you I could never run a marathon!"

Keep that from happening by setting realistic goals. First, understand and accept the fact that you're in no shape to run a marathon today. So add to your list a few short-term goals designed to lead you to the completion of the big race. Start by jogging two miles. Your next goal might be five miles. Then a 10K race. After you've achieved that short-term goal, how about working toward a mini-marathon? You'll feel excitement and exhilaration with the completion of each of these levels of achievement. You'll become inspired and more motivated than ever to run that marathon.

## SHORT-TERM GOALS BUILD CONFIDENCE

The best confidence builders of all are short-term goals. They play a crucial role in our success by giving us experience in setting and successfully meeting our long-term goals. Short-term goals can also be used to cut any unmanageable or unwieldy project down to size. We can divide and conquer any big task by separating it into smaller pieces. With the completion of each piece comes the realization of a short-term goal.

However, the fact that goals are short-term doesn't necessarily mean they are easily accomplished. Short-term refers only to the time it takes to accomplish each one, not to the amount of effort invested in it. What a rush we get when we successfully tackle and complete a short-range goal. Our self-motivation kicks into high gear as the actualization of this goal elevates us to a higher plane and affirms our vision.

Once that happens, the most amazing transformation takes place. We start seeing new goals we didn't know even existed. Goal-setting creates more opportunities than we ever imagined.

It's no secret that women who crystallize their goals perform better than women who don't. Women with strong goal-setting techniques not only finish the race, they also finish it strong.

Here's an opportunity to begin setting your short- and long-term goals. Look at the vision statement you completed in Chapter 9 and read it again. What will it take for you to realize your vision?

On the worksheet on the next page, list each specific action to get you there. State each step clearly and in positive terms so there are no mixed messages about what not to do. The whole purpose of this exercise is to improve your life, not to rehash the things that caused you pain in the past.

Our goals must be attainable, easy to visualize, and in line with our personalities. They must also be within our reach or else they're just empty air and bloated promises.

# GOALS WILL GET ME THERE!

## LONG-RANGE GOALS:

_____

_____

_____

_____

## SHORT-RANGE GOALS:

_____

_____

_____

_____

_____

_____

This doesn't mean, however, that we have to set mediocre or common goals. Goals must always provide challenge and opportunity. They might even provide adventure.

The purpose of a goal is to keep us moving forward. Momentum is created every time we complete one step and move on to the next. We feel successful, smart, full of pride, and ripe with increased energy. Hence, our action plan has to include a number of short-term goals. These are easier to accomplish and keep us from feeling discouraged waiting for the big one to bear fruit. It's dangerous to feel discouraged. We could end up tossing the entire goal list into the circular file with today's trash! That's self-defeating.

## SEE YOURSELF AS A SUCCESS

Visualizing your goals helps immensely. If a promotion is what you're after, picture yourself behind your new desk and engaged in some specific activity characterizing that new position. Picture how you would do things differently from the person who currently holds that position. If your goal is health-related, visualize a healthier, shapelier, more heart-smart you. Goal-setting is the strongest force for generating the self-motivation necessary to lead us to our vision.

Understand that all goals are not created equal. Each has a life span of its own. Some goals are more important than others. Some are easily attainable, while others require greater effort. Some necessitate a change in our attitudes or behavior. Others are more difficult to define but are still necessary to get us where we're going.

## DON'T STOP NOW!

The biggest hurdle to completing our goals successfully is the lack of self-discipline. What causes many women to fail is not limited intellect or skill but lack of concentration and the energy necessary to stick to their goals. Some women have no problem defining their goals, but never move forward to achieve them. They become sidetracked and fall far short of their ambitions.

This is exactly why we need to put our goals in writing. The act of writing down our goals is a commitment to ourselves. It represents the first step in making our goals tangible and real, rather than keeping them as ideas floating around in some amorphous form.

We need to start strong, stay strong, and finish strong, never allowing our desire for quick gratification to interfere with the successful completion of our goals.

# NEVER QUIT ON A WORTHWHILE GOAL

In December 1996, I accepted a television assignment that sent me to Sarajevo in Bosnia, a city ravaged and raped by four years of war and genocide. During these years, television sent us powerful images of destruction, death, and devastation so horrific that Americans pushed our government to get involved and help save the people of Bosnia. Our government responded by offering all sides in the battle a neutral place to talk peace. They chose Dayton, Ohio, thousands of miles from the Bosnian battleground. In 1995, Wright-Patterson Air Force Base played host to the delegates from the warring countries, who finally hammered out a successful peace agreement to end the slaughter—an agreement now known as the Dayton Peace Accord.

One year later, on the first anniversary of the signing of the peace accord, I was sent to Bosnia to report on a group of Dayton citizens who were traveling on a friendship mission, offering Bosnians a gift of hope. Our TV crew consisted of three members—another reporter, our videographer, and me. We shared the goal of returning to Dayton in ten days' time with a dozen stories and a half-hour documentary portraying the plight of the Bosnian people.

The assignment proved difficult and dangerous. Initially we worried only about the massive number of landmines still buried throughout that troubled country and about snipers who were refusing to accept the end of the war. Unexpectedly, those problems turned out to be the least of our worries.

The city is smashed and so is the economy. Virtually every building in Sarajevo has been hit by bombs or scarred by bullets. People live in homes that would be condemned in the United States.

Balkan winters are known to be harsh, and this one proved no different. After riding more than seven hours through the mountains, we stepped off our rented bus and into a foot of snow. I stayed with a host family of Serbian doctors—husband, wife, and son—who offered me the best of whatever they had. I slept on the living room sofa, which ordinarily belonged to the son. It was bitterly cold. Gas rattled through the pipes to bring heat inconsistently. Water came in two short bursts daily. It was four days before I could have more than a sponge bath in the sink.

Few people speak English to offer directions to weary travelers, and there are no salt trucks and plows to clear the icy streets. Just getting around was very difficult.

Everywhere we turned in this decimated city, we found a poignant story worth telling, but our goal of completing our assignment was in serious danger. The airlines had lost the bulk of our television equipment on the way to Bosnia. Here we were, surrounded by the stories we needed to tell, but we couldn't find our voice. Although we had managed to save the camera because my videographer kept it by his side, everything else we needed to tape our stories was gone—no batteries, no battery charger, no lights, no microphones, and no cassette tapes.

Not wanting to let our dream die, we spent a fortune on long-distance calls trying to find anyone who could lend us the equipment we needed in a hurry. The days ticked by as we struggled to find replacement gear. I was glad I'd thought to bring my home video camera. While not of the best broadcast quality, it was better than nothing.

Then we got a call from CBS News. They had managed to come up with just enough television gear for us to scrape by in Sarajevo; however, they needed it returned in two days. Two days, to do all we had to do! We became overwhelmed. All three of us had stories we wanted to shoot. Whose would we do and which would we leave out?

At first we just sat forlornly, our heads reeling. We were confused because we had to regroup, but soon we realized we had to set new plans to reach our goal. We needed to move together as one to get the most from our limited resources. Otherwise, we'd be working at cross-purposes.

We made a list of all the stories we wanted to do and prioritized them by voting on each. It soon became apparent which stories would take precedence. Together, we set our short-term goals for the two days of video shooting. As we achieved each goal, we ticked it off the list. Always moving forward, we pressed on and managed to accomplish everything on the list. Although we came back to the States with fewer stories than we desired, the result was more than we had expected. With what little we had we were able to create a moving tribute to the people of Sarajevo and the visitors from Dayton who wanted so desperately to offer their hands in friendship.

Other people might have thrown up their hands at the difficulty of trying to reach such challenging and changing goals, but we refused to give up. After a bit of reshuffling of the deck, the cards we came up with provided challenge, opportunity, and the adventure of a lifetime. We achieved our assignment by setting and completing all our goals.

# CHAPTER 11

## STEP NINE:
## BUILD YOUR REPUTATION
## ON CHARACTER

*"To keep your character intact you cannot stoop to filthy acts. It makes it easier to stoop the next time."*

—Katharine Hepburn

Melissa's vision and ultimate dream was to become Miss America. Unlike the millions of other Miss America wanna-bes in the United States, this young woman had a real shot at winning the title. Petite, blonde, beautiful, and talented, Melissa Bradley was the gal everyone in high school admired and tried to emulate. She lived a golden life, and it seemed as if she could do nothing wrong. A swimming champion, she also excelled in her studies, ultimately graduating magna cum laude from Ashland College.

Throughout high school, Melissa won honor after honor,

including a number of teenage beauty titles. But what she wanted more than anything in life was to become Miss America. It was her dream, her driving force, her vision for the future. Every goal she set and every step she took was designed to lead her to that crown—until she did something unbelievably stupid.

I met Melissa in 1996 as she spoke before a group of high school students in Ohio. We were both scheduled to speak that day. Melissa took the podium first. As I waited for my turn, I listened intently to what she was saying. I watched with amazement as she candidly revealed the most painful experience of her life to these young people, with the hope they would not make the same mistake she had. I felt her shame and embarrassment as she exposed bravely in public what most people would not admit to even in private. Her story serves as a warning to all of us to do as she says and not as she did.

Melissa told us she suffered her lapse of character in college where everyone expected her to excel as she always had in the past. She says she grew tired of being "Polly Perfect" and fell in with a group of gals who liked to take chances. They dared her to steal something. It could have been part of an initiation or just an adventure, but whatever the reason, Melissa decided to step away from her Miss Perfection image for one moment and take a chance. It was apparently the only thing in life she tried that she had no talent for. Melissa was arrested.

That one impetuous act tarnished her golden girl image, which had glistened for years. Melissa told us she found her courage in short supply in the days and weeks following her arrest, and she felt her dreams of becoming Miss America were all but over. But her dad, who lay ill in the hospital, told her to keep her head held high and understand that even in the wake of this blight on her character, she was nevertheless a young woman who still possessed good values. He urged her not to let one rash act rob her of the dreams she had worked a lifetime to accomplish.

Melissa took her father's advice that day and became renewed. As Miss Ohio 1985, she traveled to Atlantic City. Knowing she would not be able to leave her past misdeed behind, she carried more baggage than the other candidates, yet she was determined to compete.

Her dream began to unravel one hour before her private interview with the judges. CNN Television broke the story of Melissa's private scandal. Her life was now an open book on the nightly newscasts and in newspapers across the country. Instead of being regarded as a kid whose prank went sour, she was quickly gaining a notoriety that would be hard to live down. Still, she refused to fold up her tent and go home. She fought on, realizing that the judges had come to know everything there was to know about her. On the final night of competition, Melissa amazingly made the first cut. Chosen as one of the cherished top ten, she stood just two steps away from her vision of becoming Miss America.

After the final talent and swimsuit competitions, the judges narrowed down the contenders for the crown to five. Melissa was still in the running. She had done her best. Tension filled the auditorium, and soft murmurs of nervous conversation rolled from aisle to aisle as the audience wondered who would be the next Miss America.

The master of ceremonies began to call out the names and states of the runners-up. But something unusual happened when he reached the announcement of first runner-up—the young woman who would become Miss America if for any reason the winner could not fulfill her duties. He became visibly flustered. Apparently something unprecedented had happened; there appeared to be a tie for first place, and the judges needed more time to whittle down the results.

Intrigued by her story and eager for more details about the outcome of the competition, I called Melissa at her home several months after our joint speaking engagement. She graciously offered the information I desired.

She told me her heart had sunk to her knees when she heard the judges needed more time. To this day, she suspects she was indeed the number one choice for Miss America, but she will never know for sure. According to several of her sources, the pageant folks decided they might not be able to ride out the selection of a Queen with a conviction for shoplifting. The pageant had just lived through the Vanessa Williams debacle, in which Miss America was dethroned after racy pictures from her early modeling days surfaced for all the world to see. According to Melissa, the pageant people didn't want even a hint of scandal surrounding the new titleholder. After much delay and some uncomfortable moments on the stage, the new Miss America was crowned, a young Mormon woman from Utah, obviously a far safer choice.

Today, Melissa Bradley Buchanon is a spokesperson for Ohio's None for Under 21 Campaign, which urges kids to say no to alcohol and drugs. She spends many of her days counseling young people, showing them by her real-life example how character, which takes years to build, can be torn down with incredible swiftness.

## BUT MOM, SHE DARED ME!

Melissa is not alone. Many of us have things in our past of which we're not proud. A less-than-crowning moment for one of my girlfriends came at the tender age of ten. Our mothers absolutely forbade us to wear lipstick. Of course, that only increased our desire to paint our mouths saucy pink for all the world to see. Fearing my mother's wrath, I grudgingly obeyed.

My girlfriend obeyed too, until the day she walked into the five-and-ten-cent store downtown with some older girls she desperately wanted to impress. They belonged to a much faster group than we did, and she was willing to do anything to get their approval. I stood across the aisle and watched what was happening.

"To be our friend," they said, "you must prove your loyalty by taking something from the store." With those words, they pressured her into doing what she knew was wrong. I walked over and tried to talk her out of it, but she succumbed.

I followed her with my eyes as she walked up to the counter while the other girls distracted the salesperson. She was ashamed and frightened, but not wanting to lose favor with her new friends, she took a lipstick. She told me later her heart was beating so hard and fast she was sure everyone in the store could hear it. She prayed her mom would never find out.

The next day the girls pushed her further. We were in the local drug store sharing a vanilla Coke when the other girls came striding in. Once again they dared her to take something. She did. It was easier the second time. She didn't have to stoop as low because she had already lowered herself the day before. She walked over to the school supplies and clumsily pocketed a small spiral notebook that sold for fifteen cents. Not able to bring herself to steal anything of value, she somehow thought the inexpensive notebook would lessen the sin.

This time the store owner spotted her. He called her mother, apologizing for being the bearer of the bad news that her much-beloved and trusted daughter was a thief. Her mother was waiting for her as soon as she walked through the door. One look at her mother's face told my friend how much trouble she was in. She began to cry fat, ugly tears of humiliation. Without offering an explanation, she shamefacedly presented the offending notebook.

She told me she would have preferred a spanking to what she got—the knowledge of how deeply her uncharacteristic actions had wounded every member of her family. Her mother expressed her disappointment and shame, and then, without hesitation, marched her right back downtown with the stolen notebook in hand. She insisted the right thing was to pay for the notebook with fifteen cents from the girl's piggy bank and to offer an apology to the store owner.

With her mom by her side, she walked into the drug store. The owner looked very sad, and my friend began to squirm with embarrassment as her eyes met his. The owner spoke of how disappointed he was, having believed for years that she was an honest little girl. How could she do this to her family, he asked.

She wanted to die of embarrassment that awful day, and looking back she now understands why this was one of the most important days of her young life. That moment in time helped form her character from that day forward. If the incident had been ignored or swept under the rug, or if the owner had decided to look the other way because it was only a fifteen-cent notebook, her lapse of character might have become a normal way for her to behave.

My friend never tried anything like that again and never supported anyone else who did. The event was the first step in forming the code of ethics she lives by today.

# CREATE A PERSONAL CODE OF ETHICS

Character is moral strength combined with reputation. It's the kind of consistent behavior you display no matter what the circumstances. If you never back down from a challenge, people see you as having strong character. Conversely, a woman who never accepts responsibility for her actions has weak character. And a woman who lies, steals, or cheats has no character at all.

Life would be a lot easier if we could inherit character as part of our DNA make-up, but we can't. Character takes years to develop. We build it by overcoming adversity and confronting our fears. There is no easy way to acquire it. Trouble and experience are the best teachers.

However, we can speed up the process of developing good character by creating a strong code of ethics for ourselves. We can consider this code our own personal bill of rights, which establishes what we will and won't do to get ahead. Simply put, a code of ethics is a list of values that each of us considers important to her future development. It becomes the set of rules from which we operate.

Remember the movie *A Few Good Men* starring Tom Cruise, Demi Moore, and Jack Nicholson? Cruise played the part of a lawyer trying to exonerate his clients for killing another soldier while following an unofficial code of ethics.

You might not be aware of it, but you already have your own code of ethics in place—one that you may have made up as you went along. It's probably not something you consciously thought about. The code each of us has is that intangible something to help us make choices. It's the filtering process that sifts out what works best for us. Our individual codes are the yardsticks against which we measure all judgment calls and every action we take. Whenever we're asked to do something, we weigh the action, often subconsciously, by comparing it against our personal code of ethics—what we know to be right and wrong for us.

Is the code you currently operate under strong enough to make you a woman of great character?

Until now, the creation of your code may have been a passive process. It probably "created itself," and for that reason it may lack the strength you need for it to be effective. Not all the components it includes may be healthful or positive. Continual negative thinking, for example, could have tainted your code, thereby keeping you from weighing every decision in a truly healthful light. A poor code of ethics results in poor decisions. Our character suffers when we operate from a base of weakness rather than strength.

## ASSESSING YOUR VALUE SYSTEM

It's time to start taking a more active role in determining the values that make up our ethical codes.

On the next worksheet, list the values and beliefs you intend to operate under for the rest of your life. Make them morally strong. From my personal perspective, the golden rule is a good place to start. Add nothing to your value system that can weaken how you see yourself—which is your self-image—and how you feel about yourself—which is your confidence.

When we operate from a strong code of ethics, it becomes easier to make tough decisions. If someone asks you to do something, check it against your particular set of values and beliefs. If it fits in, go ahead and do it. If it doesn't, forget it.

# My PERSONAL CODE OF ETHICS

I, _____, STRONGLY BELIEVE IN _____

_____

_____

_____

_____

_____

_____

_____

I, _____, PLEDGE TO UPHOLD THE VALUES I HAVE DESCRIBED. I REALIZE THAT OPERATING WITH A STRONG PERSONAL CODE OF ETHICS TAKES COURAGE IN THE BEGINNING, BUT I REMAIN CONFIDENT IN THE KNOWLEDGE I AM DOING THE RIGHT THING.

WHEN APPLIED LIBERALLY TO MY LIFE, MY PERSONAL CODE OF ETHICS EASES THE PAINFUL PROCESS OF MAKING DECISIONS. IT ALSO AIDS ME IN FINDING FRIENDS WHO SHARE THE SAME VALUES I DO.

Notice that I said it becomes *easier* to make tough decisions, not *easy.* There's a good reason for that difference. When we care more about character than appearance, life can become somewhat more difficult. It takes courage and strength to stand up for what we believe in.

Being guided by our own strong character can seem to be the hard way of doing things, because often it may appear more expedient to take the easiest way out, like cheating on a test, bringing office supplies home from work, or telling a lie so as not to hurt someone's feelings. We rationalize our dishonest actions by saying, "But I'm not hurting anyone."

Actually, if this describes you, it hurts the most important person of all, *you.* Each dishonest step taken leads to another, even bigger one.

Good character takes extra effort. If it were easy, everybody would have it.

## INTEGRITY DEMANDS CONSISTENCY

Once we establish our code of ethics, we must follow our beliefs and values with consistency and uphold them through adversity. As the saying goes, when the going gets tough, the tough get going. In other words, the strong woman must consistently do what's right, no matter how great the effort. Successful women experience the same problems as everyone else. It's how they cope with problems and solve their dilemmas that sets them a cut above the rest of the world.

Successful people always operate with integrity, the building block of strong character. Integrity is a combination of honesty and sincerity. When you have integrity, you build your reputation on character instead of image. A good reputation is crucial to gaining respect. "A good name is more desirable than great riches; to be esteemed is better than silver or gold."[5]

Each time we open our mouths to speak, we reveal a great deal about our credibility—or lack of it. Do the words you speak ring true? Are they sincere? To be respected, admired, and successful, always say what you mean and mean what you say; that is, keep your integrity intact.

Integrity is crucial to upholding your belief system. Be sure to add it to the top of your values list. People with integrity are deadly honest with themselves as well as with others, even if it hurts.

Let's say you find yourself in a situation in which a lie is needed to cover up the ugly truth. Your coworker has opted for a new hairstyle. Instead of the professional-looking bob with bangs artfully swept to one side, she's a mass of ringlets, making her look more like a tousled moppet than the competent coworker you know she is. She loves it but you feel it's dreadful, and you're not the only one. People are laughing at her behind her back. If you value honesty, you will operate with integrity and tell her the truth, no matter what the outcome or the amount of trouble or discomfort it causes you or the other people caught up in the unpleasant situation. Of course, as a caring, supportive person, you impart that truth in a thoughtful manner designed to avoid hurting her feelings or establishing your own superiority.

Once we make integrity the core of our inner beings, we notice changes outwardly as well as inwardly. We become more confident and self-assured, because our feet are now firmly planted on a strong base of consistency. Every action we take represents our honest feelings. People will

---

5. Proverbs 22:1 (NIV).

value our opinions and respect our judgment.

As a result, we want to be careful to do nothing to harm our character. Our word is now our personal oath of honor. We need to treat it with the respect it deserves, to not make promises lightly, and to always follow through on our commitments.

Here's an example of making a commitment—perhaps to something as seemingly insignificant as promising your mother or your roommate that you will do the laundry after breakfast. Let's say that when the time arrives for you to jump in, you bail out. You decide at the last minute that you just don't feel like doing the laundry, so why bother? Instead, you sit down in front of the TV and end up wasting the time watching a mindless sitcom and snacking on junk food. You never even give the dirty laundry a second thought. Mom or your roommate comes home and finds you vegging out in front of the boob tube, a scant ten feet away from a heaping pile of unwashed clothes.

Take a good look at her face. What do you see? Initially, there's disappointment that the work isn't done. Then, if you look closely, you see something worse—disappointment in *you*. The respect you desire and your reputation both take a hit from your lack of integrity. Even if nothing is said, you and the person you let down both know the damage done to you by your lack of credibility.

Incidents like these chip away at your self-respect and your confidence, and they cause you to sabotage yourself even more. It's bad enough when someone else sets out to destroy your self-respect; it's even worse when you intentionally set yourself up to fail. Always work to maintain your integrity, because it is crucial to your identity.

In Chapter 9, we discuss the various roles you play in your life: wife, mother, worker, boss, friend, volunteer, etc.

Integrity must permeate all those roles. If you are compassionate as a person but bossy and arrogant as a company executive, you are being hypocritical. Set a standard for yourself and maintain it with consistency in all areas of your life.

## INTEGRITY VERSUS TEMPTATION

We face so many temptations in this world that it's tough not to be swept away. We may justify momentary lapses in our character by saying, "Well, everybody else is doing it." That's the time we need to dig in more than ever and uphold our values.

For example, some women are easy when it comes to sex with a new partner. Because many single women desperately want a man to like them, they feel that giving a man what he wants early in the relationship will please him. In reality, what they are doing is sacrificing respect all the way around. The woman doesn't respect her partner, because he took what she had to offer without committing to anything, even to calling her next week. He doesn't respect her because she gave away her body so easily.

"If she had sex with me this soon," he thinks, "she's probably having sex with everybody. She's nobody special." Most important, she loses respect for herself.

This is very nearly what happened to me when I was sent to interview one of the world's most outrageous and creative TV executives. When I met him, he owned a billboard company, a baseball team, and a local Atlanta television station. Today, he's a real power in the television industry.

His name is Ted Turner. He owns the Atlanta Braves and is the founder of the Turner News Network. He had the guts and the resources to shake up the television industry, creating the era of super stations to rival the big three networks, ABC, NBC, and CBS. They said it couldn't be done, but this is the man who did it.

When I met him, the Turner empire was just setting sail, as was his dream of winning the most prestigious sailing trophy in the world.

Nicknamed "Captain Courageous," Turner was racing off the picturesque waters of Newport, Rhode Island. He and his teammates were competing for the world-famous America's Cup. They had won their heat that day and were headed back to shore. My assignment was to meet Turner at the pier and get an interview.

I was waiting for him when his impressive yacht docked. My heart beat a little faster as I saw this tanned, powerful man step off the gangplank and stride over to be interviewed about the outcome of the event.

"Mr. Turner, I have a few quick questions for you," I said.

"Ask away," he replied, his restless eyes finding mine. They seemed to swallow me up like a drink of water. His aura of confidence and strength pulled me in like a paper clip to a magnet. But his arrogant self-assurance made me nervous.

The interview went well, and when it ended he asked me if I would like to visit his yacht. Excited about the prospect of setting foot on this contribution to racing history, I turned to my videographer and exclaimed, "Ted Turner wants us to see his yacht. Come on!"

"Ah, Donna, I don't think I'm invited. You go ahead without me," my videographer said, chuckling. Apparently, the videographer was part of the old boys' network and knew precisely what was supposed to happen. I only wish he had shared the information with me. Physically, I was twenty-eight years old, but romantically, my growth had been severely stunted.

I argued with him for a while, but he insisted I go alone, that the invitation was extended only to me. I finally gave up. Not wanting to miss the opportunity, I strode back to Turner's side and told him I would be happy to take a tour.

Imagine my surprise as we started to lumber down a different gangplank from the one I'd seen Turner use earlier. Instead of finding myself heading toward the sleek racing vessel, I saw a yacht outfitted like a large home. I was dismayed at the change of plans, but as a less-than-affluent girl from Cape Cod who had never set foot on a yacht before, I thought, "Why not? Let's see how the other half lives!"

As I reached out to steady myself on the gangplank, I looked up at my videographer on the pier, who was encircled by some of his counterparts from the other local TV stations. They looked highly amused, obviously sharing a joke. I thought, "Oh, well," and readied myself for my entrance into high society. Little did I know that the joke was on me.

As I began walking down the gangplank, that little alarm finally went off inside my gut. You know, the one our mothers install immediately after we are born. Every time we're about to do something stupid, it goes off, sending bile racing from the liver, making us slightly nauseated with the awareness, down deep inside, that our actions could lead to trouble. But we develop a what-the-heck attitude and go ahead anyway.

Still I pressed on in my zeal to see what being rich and powerful felt like. But not wanting to be totally stupid, I did take a careful look at my surroundings, and I felt comforted by what I saw. Several members of the crew were tending to their various duties on deck. Good, I thought, there would be other people on this floating hotel.

However, any sense of security I created for myself vanished within minutes as the crew members, one by one, started leaving the boat, seeming to vanish into thin air. I guess that was the idea.

My tour began and ended in Turner's stateroom. As he pushed open the door to his private cabin, he turned and grabbed both my shoulders, pulling me into an embrace.

"I'm a Scorpio," he said huskily. "You're a Gemini, aren't you?" I was amazed, both by what was happening and by what he was saying. Even though horoscope signs in the seventies doubled as pick-up lines, I was disarmed by this man's apparent clairvoyance, as my birth date, June 10, makes me a Gemini to the core. Maybe all Geminis are as naïve as I am. Call me "Clueless from Cape Cod," I was really not prepared for what happened next.

Turner pulled me tightly into him, tumbling against the edge of the bunk. You couldn't have slipped a piece of newscopy between us. His eyes caught mine and he put his hand on my chin, lightly lifting my face to meet his. Though the yacht didn't move, I felt as if I were drifting away from the dock as he pressed on with a hard and passionate kiss—a kiss that shook me from head to toe. I felt a rush of lust as my knees grew weak. That's when I began to feel ashamed—ashamed I had been operating from a naïve code of ethics and sending out the wrong message. The situation was becoming too hot for me to handle.

Turner was a gentleman, however, for when I asked him to stop, he did. Within seconds, I recovered my composure. I felt cheap and used, but in this case, I couldn't blame him. All the warning signs were there and I had chosen to ignore them. I should have turned around and walked off the gangplank when the first alarm sounded in my gut. Instead, I sacrificed my integrity. My actions were not reflective of the values and ethics I truly believed in.

But there's a funny side to the story. Turner threw out one last shot as I stumbled out of the stateroom portal.

"I'm starting up the fourth largest TV network," he said, "and you could be one of my anchorwomen."

"Yeah, right!" I returned fire, never believing for a moment that anyone could go up against the network biggies and win.

As I breathlessly rushed up the gangplank and onto the pier, I ran smack into my videographer, almost knocking the wind out of him. The rest of the photographers and reporters he had been laughing with earlier were walking away, shaking their heads in disappointment.

"What's going on?" I asked my videographer, who was standing there holding onto a fistful of dollars. "What's that for?" I asked.

"Well," he said, "I bet them you were ignorant, but not stupid, and as soon as you figured out what kind of a tour you were taking, you'd coming running off that yacht in no time flat."

Had I lived then by the code of ethics I have today, this melodrama on the high seas would never have made it past the first act, and my character would not have been placed in jeopardy. Ted Turner did not drag me on to his yacht; I went willingly. What I should have done, to be true to myself, was to say, "No, thank you. I'll pass." I should have set boundaries. It was a powerful lesson.

Like the imaginary line drawn in the desert sand by President George Bush during the Persian Gulf War, our personal codes of ethics help us establish boundaries to let people know how far they can go. They also outline what we will and won't do to get ahead in this world.

Never compromise your boundaries. Never compromise yourself. As a mason fortifies a wall with well-placed stones, a smart woman fortifies her character with integrity.

# CHAPTER 12

---

# STEP TEN:
# DIG IN WITH
# DETERMINATION

---

*"You may have to fight a battle more than once to win it."*

—*Margaret Thatcher*

It was the worst thing that could possibly happen to any runner racing for Olympic gold. Her feet bruised and swollen, Gail Devers was told by the doctors they might have to amputate.

A U.S. track and field athlete, Gail has spent her entire life sprinting her way to success. A stand-out distance runner in high school, she switched to sprinting, becoming the California state champion in 1984 in the 100-meter dash and the 100-meter hurdles.

Her efforts won her an athletic scholarship and the attention of coach Bob Kersee, the husband of another famous runner, Jackie Joyner-Kersee. Gail's determination, combined with Bob's coaching, led her to a U.S.-record-setting sprint in the 100-meter hurdles and a spot on the 1988 Olympic team.

Thought to be the closest thing to a sure bet, Gail was expected to bring home the gold in Seoul, South Korea, but she did not fare well. A host of ailments began to plague her before the starter's gun signaled the first race. Determined to get through the games, she did her best, but her performance was disappointing. Doctors examined her and had difficulty coming up with a diagnosis for her expanding list of problems, which were now sapping her strength and stealing her talent.

At first they thought Gail's determination had overtaken her common sense, that she had trained too hard and over-taxed her athletic body. But this was not the case. Doctors finally identified the culprit robbing her of her athletic prowess. In 1990, Gail was diagnosed with Graves disease, a hyperthyroid condition. Gail required immediate treatment.

Doctors recommended the standard beta-blocker medication, but with the Olympic flame still fanning the fire of her desire, Gail refused. She knew the Olympic committee deemed the drug an illegal substance for its athletes. So she opted instead for radiation treatment.

Her hopes soared as the radiation destroyed part of her thyroid, thereby improving her overall condition. But then came the unexpected. Her once-fleet feet, which had served her so well, began to swell and became infected. Doctors told Gail they might have to amputate. She fell apart, her determination severely affected by overwhelming pain and desperation. At this point she couldn't walk, let alone run.

For somebody who lacks determination, the story could have ended there, but not for Gail and her coach, Bob.

As I watched the movie of her life, *Run for the Dream: The Gail Devers Story*, I was moved to tears by the courage of Gail and her coach, both determined to get her stubborn and sick feet working again. Just getting up from her wheelchair often proved a marathon event, her body exhausted by the radiation treatments and the disease.

They got a break when the swelling in her feet subsided shortly after the radiation treatments were finished. Gail became inspired and determined to run again, and Bob began pushing her hard. They set little goals at first.

I watched as Bob pushed her wheelchair out to the track. He lined it up at one of the starting positions and then took a small stick and placed it about a foot from the wheelchair in front of her. Gail began to cry as she momentarily lost faith, feeling this part of her life was surely over. Bob wouldn't take no for an answer. He refused to baby her. He chose, instead, to appeal to her competitive nature.

"Just take two steps," he said. "Just make it to the stick, then you can sit down and we'll call it a day." Racked with emotional and physical pain, Gail rose unsteadily from her chair. Her feet aching, body limp, and spirits sagging, she resolutely took her first baby step, then paused and took another. The pain was immense and overwhelming, but still she moved forward. She stepped over the stick Bob had set a small distance away, brushing the top of it with the bottom of her sluggish foot. This took a Herculean effort for Gail. Her baby steps were, in reality, giant steps.

The cheers she heard that day did not come from an Olympic-sized crowd. They came from Bob, who reached out and lifted Gail high in the air, both of them shedding tears of joy. This was a major breakthrough—the doctors had said it couldn't be done. If she could do this, maybe— just maybe—she could compete in the Olympics again.

More determined than ever, she resumed daily practice. Each day Gail and her coach visited the track. Each day that stick was pushed out a bit farther. Her shambling and weak steps became more sure over the next few months. Soon she was not only walking erect but running again.

Gail resumed her track career in 1991, with a medication approved by the Olympic Committee, a medicine she will have to take for the rest of her life. In less than two years, Gail went from being seriously ill to winning Olympic gold.

At the 1992 games in Barcelona, Spain, she raced to a gold medal in the 100-meter dash. More titles and awards followed after that. In 1993, the magazine *Track and Field News* named her the U.S. Female Athlete of the Year.

In 1996 in Atlanta, Georgia, Gail finished in the gold again. Her story is a source of inspiration to us all. It exemplifies determination at its best. When her illness became the biggest obstacle of all, Gail Devers dug in, and with great personal pain and sacrifice, she hurdled it to come out a winner. She refused to listen to those who said it couldn't be done, surrounding herself, instead, with those who would fuel her determination and believe in her as she believed in herself.

## WHEN THE GOING GETS TOUGH, JUST GET GOING

Determination is that gut-wrenching feeling we get every time we face adversity. Take, for example, the marathon runner who gets a pain in her side that signals she's reaching her limit. That's the moment when she needs to dig deep inside to reach the driving force that will propel her past the pain to the finish line.

What she's digging for is determination, the tenacity to keep going while the rest of her body yells, "Stop!"

Adversity creates determination. Without difficulty or misfortune, there is no need to become determined about anything in life.

Twice in my lifetime I've had the misfortune of having taxi cab drivers spit on me—once in New York City, and again in Frankfurt, Germany. The first time, my wallet had been stolen in the Big Apple, and as it turned out I had exactly enough money to pay the cab fare from the hotel to the airport. That left nothing for a tip. I sorrowfully explained my tale of woe to the driver as I handed him the money for the fare. He picked up my luggage, threw it at me, and then spat in my face. I allowed myself to be humiliated by this man I didn't even know. I picked up my bags, and with hot tears of embarrassment pouring down my burning cheeks, I miserably made my way to the gate to catch my plane.

Instead of facing this small adversity with determination, I adopted the "poor little me" attitude. That picture changed in 1996, sixteen years later, when history repeated itself—as it often does.

I was on a television assignment in Europe. After traveling twelve hours from the States I was exhausted, wanting nothing more than to reach my hotel and dive under the opulent down comforter on the bed. I left the Frankfurt baggage claim wheeling my suitcases on those wonderful little rollers and got in line for a taxi. Unbeknownst to me, the hotel was only a two-minute drive from where I stood. It was located at the entrance to the airport—a short, inexpensive run for any taxi driver who was hoping for a lucrative fare to make waiting in line worthwhile.

When I gave the taxi driver the name of the hotel, he spat on me, threw up his hands in disgust, and cursed at me in German. This happened ten more times as I made my way down the line of waiting cabs. One after another they rejected me in that ugly manner, spitting, cursing, and making obscene gestures, but still I refused to give up. It was too far to walk loaded down with suitcases; I had no choice but to hire a cab. That was the ugliest fifteen minutes of my life. However, the more rejection I encountered, the more my determination kicked in.

I searched the eyes of the remaining cab drivers, looking for a spark of kindness. Finally I found what I was desperately seeking, a gentleman with a twinkle in his eye. After I told him where I needed to go, his smile sagged, but he didn't spit or curse. I offered him a rather large tip to take me there. Even though it was less than he would have made on a trip downtown, he rewarded me with a genuine smile and packed my bags into his cab. He even apologized for the way I had been treated by his fellow cab drivers.

Instead of accepting an unacceptable situation, I reached deep inside and found the resolve necessary for me to keep going until I got what I wanted. In the face of insult and adversity, I became determined.

The more challenging our goals are in life and the more obstacles and adversity we face, the more we need the driving force of determination to move us forward. Being determined is saying, "I'm going to do it or else!" It's knowing with certainty you will achieve your goals and reach your vision, even if it means crawling over broken glass to get there.

Lauren Hutton, famous model and actress, proved her critics wrong after suffering a blow early in her long, successful career.

"They told me to fix my teeth, change my nose, even get out of the business. But I stayed, and learned, and didn't give up!"

And how about best-selling novelist Mary Higgins Clark? A young widow left with five children she needed to clothe, feed, and support, Clark also had a penchant for writing. She took a nine-to-five job to support her family, but she never stopped dreaming of literary success. Determined to be a writer, she sacrificed greatly to appease her muse. She awoke hours before her children, put her thoughts down on paper, then got the kids ready for school. After that, she'd head to the office for a full day's work. Now that's determination.

## DETERMINED WOMEN DO WHAT IT TAKES

Crawling over broken glass would have been an easy challenge compared to the adversity Hilda Spurlock has endured in her lifetime. In 1996, I was looking for a victim to best illustrate the face of domestic violence for a televised report. One look at Hilda's face told me I had found the right woman.

"I hid what was happening to me until I couldn't hide it no more," Hilda revealed unashamedly to the TV audience, many of whom couldn't believe what they were seeing.

Ten years before, Hilda had finally found the courage to leave the husband who'd been abusing her mentally and physically during their years of marriage. The court granted her a divorce, but that didn't stop her abuser from pursuing her. Saying, "If I can't have you, nobody else will!" Hilda's ex-husband picked up a double-barreled shotgun, tucked it neatly under her chin, pulled the trigger, and blew away half of her face.

Hilda survived the shooting, but her face didn't. Half her jaw is gone, ripped away by the force of the blast that also shattered her left check. Her toothless mouth appears as a jagged uneven slash on what remains of her face. Mercifully, she didn't lose her eyes.

But don't waste time feeling sorry for Hilda. She is one of the happiest and most courageous women I know. She refuses to remain a victim and never feels sorry for herself. In fact, she accomplished what many women fear to try. She helped prosecutors send her estranged husband to prison. Ironically, he died while serving time for nearly killing her. Free of the man who violently abused her, Hilda never looks back. When she looks in the mirror today, she sees her scarred face as an opportunity to enlighten others about the lasting horrors of domestic violence.

Over the course of ten years, it cost a million dollars, countless operations, and indescribable pain to put Hilda back together again. Doctors softened her harsh countenance by replacing her missing jaw with her hip bone. And by moving muscles from her thigh to her face, they restored her smile. For the first time in a decade, Hilda can chew her food, thanks to a new set of false teeth specially designed for her misshapen mouth. To the casual onlooker, Hilda now looks like a woman who has had a slight stroke, instead of the object of a vicious domestic violence assault.

Hilda made an important choice to walk away from an abusive situation and to take control of her life instead of letting it control her. In spite of the way things turned out, Hilda never doubts she did the right thing. If she had stayed with the man who was abusing her, she believes he would have done more than maim her; ultimately he would have killed her.

Even in those dark days, she never doubted there would be a brighter tomorrow. She was determined to have a full, meaningful life, and she overcame misfortune and adversity to find it.

# BUT IT'S A MAN'S JOB

Jaruth Durham-Jefferson is a strong, determined African-American woman who became a success in spite of a double dose of discrimination—as a black and as a woman. She and I were the speakers of choice at a mother-daughter banquet in Dayton in 1996. When I wasn't doing the talking, I sat back and listened to what she had to say. I became inspired by the story of how this professional woman found great success in a career that had been considered a "man's job."

Her story truly begins the year her husband died. Widowed at thirty-two, with a nine-year-old son to raise, Jaruth needed to make some big decisions about the future. One night as her TV set flickered in the pale evening light, Jaruth watched intently as an employment ad for the Dayton police force came into focus. The message she saw emblazoned across her tiny screen made her angry: "Dayton police are looking for a few good men."

While she sat and watched the ad roll across the small screen, she reflected on her recent loss and the discrimination she was now facing as a widow with a young boy to raise. Just days before she spotted the ad asking for "a few good men," Jaruth's refrigerator had conked out, and she had headed down to the local appliance store. Within minutes she was turned down for credit. The reason? As a new widow, she had no credit of her own, even though she had often been the one paying the family bills. Her husband had loads of good credit, but according to the appliance salesperson, her husband had taken their good credit rating with him when he died.

That's one reason the Dayton police employment ad hit her so hard. It was just more people telling her what she couldn't do. It was hard enough for a widow to find a well-paying job, but the thought of an employer suggesting that because she was a woman she couldn't have an opportunity to better her life angered her beyond reason.

Jaruth decided it was time to show the police what a good woman could do. Determined to win the job, she went downtown to take the police entrance exam. She was surprised but pleased to find other women there who were also determined to make the grade. Jaruth scored well on the test and entered the police academy against the wishes of her mother, aunts, and cousins.

"Is that any job for a woman?" they wanted to know. Jaruth says they talked themselves blue trying to persuade her not to make policing her career. They thought she had gone quite mad from grief after the death of her husband. "Why would you want to be a police officer? That's a man's job." But Jaruth coolly informed them she knew what she was doing, boldly taking her first step into a career in law enforcement and becoming one of the first women police officers in the city of Dayton, Ohio.

It was a career move that proved to be anything but easy. Her young son had to become self-reliant very quickly. After dinner they would sit at the dining room table, spread out their respective school books, and study together.

Jaruth and her son made many sacrifices as she pursued a better life filled with opportunity for both of them. What a wonderful role model her son had in his mother—a woman who was passionate about her beliefs and determined to be a success.

Jaruth currently holds the rank of major, a prestigious position won after years of pounding the beat on the gritty streets, working as an undercover cop busting pimps, prostitutes, and drug dealers, and negotiating to free hostages held at gunpoint. Her rise through the ranks was rapid.

She had set her sights high and used determination at every turn. Her vision is to become a chief of police one day.

When the force failed to provide the education necessary to take her to the next level, she showed initiative by paying for it herself. During breakfast with me one morning, Jaruth reiterated this point: "Women can't always wait to be selected for the training necessary to do the job, so pay for it yourself. It's a valuable investment in your future."

Today, Jaruth is a proud grandmother of five. She is also a much sought-after candidate for chief of police in cities throughout the nation. She remains determined to succeed despite the fact that she has more than a few gray hairs.

"Donna, age is not a barrier," she says. "If one can do it, all can do it."

Jaruth told me she inherited her strong-willed determination from her mother, who dished out old-fashioned homilies along with dinner. With advice such as, "Things done in half are never done right," Jaruth's cherished mother taught her the importance of respect, dignity, honor, and determination. "Determination and the willingness to work toward the goal will get you there."

Jaruth found success in a simple formula: establish your vision, set your goals, and apply determination to achieve them.

As her mother said, and as she now echoes, "Whatever you do, be proud to put your stamp on it."

## I'D LIKE TO ORDER SOME DETERMINATION, PLEASE

Jaruth's story is a wonderful example of how you can find determination when your own may seem to be in short supply. First, focus your attention on the problem at hand.

Then, apply sustained energy and effort to solve it. You not only achieve your desired outcome, you also develop strength of character. Character is the natural by-product of the struggle between determination and adversity.

Like a runner, set your sights straight ahead and keep your eyes focused on the finish line. You won't get anywhere looking over your shoulder to see who or what's creeping up on you. Continually glancing back makes you lose ground. Instead, apply concentration and focus clearly on the end of the race.

Olympic track star Florence Griffith-Joyner has a credo she lives by: "Believe . . . Achieve . . . Succeed."

Have you ever seen someone juggle plates in the circus, or—if you're old enough—on the *Ed Sullivan Show*? You know the one I'm talking about—the performer who sets an ordinary dinner plate spinning on top of a ten-foot pole. He gets about six poles and plates spinning, and he must keep running back and forth to keep them going, constantly moving, constantly in motion. If he fails, the plate drops to the floor in a crash.

You must have that kind of tenacity and determination to keep the plates spinning in your life, because life won't stand still for you. There is only one thing that's constant, and that's change. So if you're not moving forward with determination, guess where you're headed? You got it— you must be slipping back.

## READY, SET . . . GO!

Now is the time to change your life for the better. You have just been given ten sure-fire steps to change your life. Taking them requires commitment and accountability.

It took the completion of all ten steps for me to become truly successful and empowered—and independent rather than co-dependent. I no longer measure my success against other people's. I do what is right for me regardless of what others think of my actions. I always operate with honesty and integrity, which in turn makes life less complicated and more satisfying. However, my success came only after a few false starts.

For years, I believed I had "arrived" and that I was truly a woman of power, but I was only fooling myself. There was always this nagging little voice in the back of my mind telling me I was not what I appeared to be. That little voice was right. People saw me as a success because my self-image had greatly improved, but inside I was still a work in progress.

It took one final test of my abilities to put me over the top and make me firmly believe in my talents, my abilities, and myself. I needed to wrangle an invitation to the White House to talk with the most powerful leader in the world. That was in 1990.

## EXCUSE ME, MR. PRESIDENT?

"Can you free up some time next week to come to Washington? You're invited to the White House for a meeting with President George Bush."

I couldn't believe the call had finally come. I was being summoned to the most prestigious address in the nation for what turned out to be one of the more exciting adventures in my broadcasting career.

My journey to Pennsylvania Avenue was fraught with obstacles. Foremost was the fact that I work in a city ranking fifty-third among more than 200 television markets across the country. I had to plan my strategy to gain access to the president carefully, because I knew he wasn't going to waste time in a fireside chat with a small player when

he could invite the media representing the top ten markets, such as Boston, Chicago, New York, and San Fran-
cisco.

I launched a letter-writing campaign, first to George, then
to Barbara, then to Dan and Marilyn Quayle. I told them
all that I would like to interview them. Ideally, I wanted
the president, but I would take what I could get. Hope
dimmed as weeks went by with no word from the White
House. Then my chances slipped from slim to none as I
watched the troops massing for the build-up at the start of
the Persian Gulf War. The president now had a lot more on
his mind than granting an interview to an anchor from a
TV station in Dayton, Ohio. Still, I wasn't ready to give up.
I was more determined than ever to get to the White House,
especially when the biggest news of the Bush administration was breaking.

"What should I do next?" I wondered, temporarily putting my quest on the back burner while I fulfilled other
obligations—one of which, as fate would have it, ended up
paving my way to the White House.

I was scheduled to deliver a speech to what I thought
would be a small group at the convention center. It was my
understanding that I would be providing motivation for a
group of thirty career women, but I was wrong. Somewhere
along the line, communication got tangled, and I arrived
to find more than 300 women waiting to be inspired. A
group that large takes some additional preparation. So I
did what Abraham Lincoln might have done. I grabbed an
envelope, sat down, and began to sketch out a more suitable speech.

As I was doing so, I heard someone mention that I would
be the second speaker of the evening. It was already 7:00
P.M. and I needed to return to the TV station by 9:15 to prepare for my broadcast. Realizing that this event was shap-

ing up to be a long night, I did something I had never done before and will never do again. Just call me "prima Donna."

"Could you please put me on the program first?" I asked the woman in charge, explaining that I had many important duties back at the TV station. She graciously agreed to my arrogant request. My mistake was not asking the name of the speaker I had just bumped into second place.

I was instructed to enter the hall from the rear. Marching to the drumbeat of the local high school band, I led the parade of dignitaries entering from my side of the auditorium. The other speaker would do the same from the other side.

As I made my way briskly into the cavernous room, I glanced to the other side to make sure I was lined up properly. At that moment I caught just a glimpse of the other speaker. I couldn't see him clearly, but he appeared very distinguished, and he looked vaguely familiar, like somebody famous.

"Oh, no, it can't be!" I said as I got a closer look. A friendly twinkle in his pale eyes lit up the shy, rather nondescript face, and by the time I reached the podium and turned, there I stood, face to face with a bona fide hero, famous astronaut and U.S. Senator John Glenn—the speaker I had just bumped down in the program.

"Horrors!" I thought, as I began frantically signaling the chairwoman's attention to try to undo the damage I had done. I looked like a sailor trying to flag a message to a passing ship.

"We have two special guests with us today," the woman cooed, "and one of them is so very important we are asking her to speak first. Senator Glenn, you'll have to wait. Ms. Jordan needs to get back to work to fulfill her many duties."

I wanted to die of sheer embarrassment. Fortunately, the senator took the slight with good humor. After presenting my speech, I decided to break curfew and stay another half hour to hear Senator Glenn speak. As I sat back and watched him step up to the podium to make his remarks, I was stunned by the brilliance of a thought passing through my brain. This famous man could be the answer to the problem I had been wrestling with for weeks.

Minutes after he concluded his speech, I drew the senator away from his fans, who had rushed the stage and surrounded him. After exchanging pleasantries, I got down to business.

"Senator, I need to get to the White House to interview President Bush. Could you please intercede for me?"

"Wrong house!" he said with a chuckle. "After all, I am a Democrat."

"Ah yes," I said, "but you're also a legend, a hero astronaut. Surely, they'll listen to you."

"No promises, Donna, but I'll see what I can do."

I thanked Senator Glenn and walked away more determined than ever to get to the White House. You never know where your next bright idea will come from, and this experience had just given me a terrific one.

Grabbing my phone the next morning, I speed-dialed every Republican I could think of who'd have access to the White House and asked them to intercede on my behalf. To this day, I don't know exactly who carried my flag into battle, but I will always be grateful to those who did.

Within two weeks I got the call. I was going to the White House!

I was one of only eleven television journalists selected to interview the president that day—a special media conference for regional reporters instead of our national counterparts, who visit the White House on a daily basis.

"Why did you select me?" I asked after accepting the invitation to be part of this fortunate group.

"We've invited journalists from the top ten TV markets . . . and you," replied the White House communications staffer seriously. Then she began to laugh. "Let's just say the squeaky wheel gets the grease. By the way, the Administration would like to know how you managed to elicit bipartisan support."

I believe Senator Glenn might have been among those who'd graciously come through.

Although I had made it into the delegation, the staffer made no promises that the president would call on me. "He makes the choice, I don't," she said.

So I questioned her on the best way to get the president's attention to increase the odds of his selecting me.

"Well, the protocol is . . ." she began. I stopped her in mid-sentence.

"I understand about protocol. That's not what I'm asking. I want some inside information. Is there anything I can do or say that will make the president call on me?"

"I can't believe it. Nobody's ever asked me this before," she replied, chuckling. She went on. "Okay. What do you look like?" I explained that I was a petite blonde.

"That's great," she said. "Take a seat in the front row, right in front of the president, and be sure to wear his favorite colors."

"Red, white, and blue?" I guessed.

"You got it. Do that and I can almost guarantee he will call on you."

Terrific! Armed with a game plan and a wardrobe seemingly designed by Betsy Ross, I hopped a plane for Washington.

A bright and sunny day welcomed my videographer and me to our nation's capital. It had been years since I'd felt this challenged and excited about an assignment. I caught up with the ten other journalists in a White House foyer. Making polite conversation, we milled about waiting for the big event. I spotted a woman across the room who was actively trying to catch my eye. As her sweeping glance took in my patriotic outfit from head to toe, she began softly chuckling.

"Let me guess," she exclaimed after she'd cut her way through the crowded room heading straight for me. "You must be Donna from Dayton!"

"You bet I am," I replied, "and I'm ready to question the president."

"Good thing, because there's big news. The president has fired the Air Force Chief of Staff for shooting off his mouth about our military's battle plans against Iraq. This is no longer a regional media conference. It is now open to everybody—ABC, CBS, NBC, CNN, *Time*, *Newsweek*, and the rest of the national and international media. However, you eleven journalists are still responsible for asking the primary questions."

What a break. Determination got me here and now it would be determination giving me the greatest advantage. It was no longer important to have the president call on me whenever I managed to catch his eye. It became imperative that I be the first person to ask Mr. Bush the question of the day: "Why did you really fire the Air Force Chief of Staff?"

She told me the president would offer a statement on the story at the beginning of the media conference but would refuse to answer any more questions about it. I knew I couldn't let it go at that.

I pondered what I could possibly do to get the jump on the more experienced reporters from the bigger markets. I found the answer by simply asking the staffer. "What do I do if the president refuses to call on me?"

"The protocol is . . . ." One quick look at my face told her not to go there again. "Oh, right, I'm talking to Donna from Dayton! Okay." Then she whispered conspiratorially, "Here's what you have to do. Wait until the president makes his official statement, then when he starts to ramble at the end, raise your hand and call 'Mr. President,' then slip your hand down to cover your mouth, look embarrassed, and say, 'Oh, excuse me.'"

"You mean interrupt him on purpose?" I asked with supreme incredulity.

"Yep, he'll call on you next. I've seen it happen before. But until now, it's happened only by accident."

I thanked her mightily for the information and spent a few quiet moments organizing my thoughts.

So here's the plan. I'm about to enter totally unfamiliar territory and take control of the media conference by interrupting the most powerful leader in the world to ask him a question he doesn't want to answer. Oh, that's a great plan. But, like it or not, that was Plan A, and there was no Plan B.

Finally, it was time to enter the auditorium, and I was determined to take the front-row seat the Bush administration staffer had pointed out, the seat right in front of the podium where reporter Helen Thomas usually sits. As the doors to the room opened, I rushed to the front and plunked myself down as quickly as possible.

Tension began to mount as we awaited the nation's chief executive. First on the docket to brief us was Secretary of Defense Dick Cheney. He strode to the podium, never cracking a smile, and told of the situation concerning the Air

Force Chief of Staff. He warned us not to ask the president any further questions on the matter. Then he began taking questions. I raised my hand repeatedly, but Cheney refused to call on me.

Determined but frustrated, I decided to pull out the heavy artillery I was saving for President Bush. After all, you really should test your weapon before you actually need to use it.

I waited until Cheney was in the middle of a convoluted answer to another reporter's question, and then I shot my hand up from my lap and bellowed, "Mr. Secretary . . . oh, excuse me!" As I pulled my hand down and demurely covered my mouth, Cheney shot me a look that cut me dead. But he did call on me next. I guess he figured, "I'd better shut her up before she interrupts me again." I asked him a question about the role the Soviets were playing in the conflict, which he conscientiously answered. That mission accomplished, it was time to meet the president.

As Mr. Bush swept in surrounded by his entourage, I looked up eagerly, desperate to draw his attention to me. His eyes scanned the audience. "Good morning, ladies and gentlemen. Nice to see you. Good morning, everyone."

I had done everything to prepare for this moment, but the next step would be up to him. He didn't let me down. The president paused two steps from the podium, looked down, smiled at me directly, and said, "Well, hello! Good morning."

"Good morning, Mr. President," I answered and smiled back. Our eyes locked for a moment. Yes! At that moment I knew with certainty the president would call on me. Now the only challenge was to get him to call on me *first* so I could be the reporter asking the big question.

All my senses went into overdrive as I became alert for

opportunity. The president began his statement, talking about why he had fired such an important military man. But he wasn't really saying much.

I listened intently as the president imparted only minimal information and then added, "This will be the only comment I will make on the subject."

Still, I was determined to get more. I waited as he brought his statement to a close. He was beginning to ramble as his staffer had predicted. This was the moment of opportunity. Timidly I began to raise my hand but hesitated midway, overwhelmed by the magnitude of what I was about to do: intentionally interrupt the President of the United States.

After several insecure tries, I decided to seize the moment, but just as my hand was beginning its ascent, I heard a rustling behind me. Oh, no. I realized I had waited too long. A booming voice came from behind my right ear. "Mister . . ." began another reporter in a deep baritone. But before he could get any further, I shot out of my seat like a missile being fired from a rocket launcher. With my right arm extended toward the ceiling, I screamed the rest of the other reporter's salutation: ". . . President!"

The president looked at both of us and smiled. "I'll call on you first," he said to the reporter behind me. Then, as his gazed shifted to me he said, "I'll take you next."

That's when I began to pray to God to make the man behind me ask a stupid question. It wasn't a nice thing to do, but it worked. It seemed that God answered my prayer. The reporter, based in L.A., asked a question about gang violence instead of concentrating on the firing of the Air Force Chief. Luckily for me, the reporter couldn't improvise and stuck to his original material instead of going for the breaking news.

I kept my hand raised by my side to remind the president I was next.

"Yes, you had a question?" he said, smiling down at me.

"Yes, sir, I do. Mr. President, could you please explain to me in more detail exactly why you fired the Air Force Chief of Staff?"

At that moment, a couple of the president's thousand points of lights must have gone out, because the wattage of his bright smile dimmed. He was seriously displeased.

"I told you, I wouldn't answer that question," he replied, and for a moment he said no more.

It was one of the longest moments of my life. I finally understood what the term "flop sweat" meant. Still, I refused to blink as the "discomfort factor" began to rise.

Then the president broke the tension by issuing the one word I had longed to hear.

"But . . . ."

That meant he was going to answer my question. And then he did, beautifully.

## ALWAYS MOVE FORWARD

By taking the lead I won the prize that important day. Not only did I get the job done in the most outstanding way possible, but I earned the envy of all my counterparts and scored big points with the TV brass at my local station.

To make that happen I had to use every one of my ten steps. I started with a vision, then set goals, and finally dug in with the driving force of determination to ensure success. Along the way I refused to listen to the people who told me I'd never get to the White House, but if by some amazing stroke of luck I did, I certainly wouldn't be able to talk with the president. I met every obstacle with courage and hurdled them with ease.

I never stopped believing in myself and my abilities. Success was mine that day—as it has been most of the days of my life—because I knew without a doubt that failure is *not* an option.

# EPILOGUE

## A FINAL NOTE

*"I tell you the truth, if you have faith as small as a mustard seed, you can say to this mountain, 'Move from here to there' and it will move. Nothing will be impossible for you."*

—*Matthew 17:20 (NIV)*

One more ingredient remains to be mixed well into your personal recipe for success, and that's a strong measure of faith. Faith is complete trust in and reliance on yourself and your ability to work through any sticky situation life hands you, because of your unquestioning belief in a higher power. For me, that means God. I recognize and respect that your idea of a higher power may differ from mine. So, as you read my words, feel free to apply my message to your own belief system.

When skies are at their darkest and you seem to experience one defeat after another, you need to be able to look to the heavens and know with certainty that the higher power in your life is in control and has a plan designed especially for you, a plan that one day will lead to your success. God will never let you down, even when you disappoint yourself.

Momentary disappointments are only that, transient, fleeting things. God looks at the big picture when we get wrapped up in the petty things in life. Sometimes, there are painful lessons each of us needs to learn to become a better, stronger person. I used to question why this was so, but I don't any more.

As I look back on my own journey in life, I know now why I experienced so many rough spots. I am stronger and smarter today because of the lessons learned in my travails and travels. I truly believe God wants me to use those times of trouble to share with other women how to avoid life's biggest disasters.

I experienced much pain on my road to success, but I am tougher, more resilient, and more talented because of it. Trusting in a higher power was a hard lesson for me to learn. It was difficult for me to take that first leap of faith, to give up control over my own life to God, but once I did, my life improved dramatically. There were many times I tried to wrest control from God, thinking I could handle this myself. But those are usually the times I found myself in hot water. Today, I trust completely in the infinite wisdom of my higher power and thank God for guiding me each and every day.

## USING FAITH TO
## FIND A HUSBAND

Strange as it sounds, my faith also brought me a new husband. After my divorce, I read a number of self-help books as I worked to wean myself of the co-dependency problems that had plagued my life thus far—problems stemming from my habit of putting other people's needs and desires before my own. One of the books that made a difference for me is *If I'm So Wonderful, Why Am I Still Single?* by Susan Page. I now own a carton of these paperbacks and hand them out to friends and anyone else who is looking to form healthy relationships with others. In the book, Page advises you to write a list of attributes describing the mate you're seeking. I wasted no time making out my list. Here it is:

- Blue eyes, black hair, and a little forelock that tumbles down on his forehead like Superman's.
- He should be of average height so I could fit snugly under his arm.
- He shouldn't smoke and must be no more than a casual social drinker.
- He must own his own business or be the CEO or the COO of a large, successful corporation.
- He must be an athlete who can ski (but not better than I can, because I want at least one sport where I could outdistance him!).
- He must have been married at least seven years . . . divorced about three (because I wanted him on an equal footing with me).
- There must be no children . . . no in-laws . . . no baggage from the previous marriage.
- He must possess a strong faith in the Lord to help me in my Christian walk.
- He should be strong yet vulnerable (tearing up at sad, emotional movies is acceptable)—a solid man who prefers substance over the sensational.
- He must be dependable and kind in his treatment of others.
- He must be a loving, exciting, and sensual lover who

wouldn't be afraid to sacrifice his own pleasure momentarily to enhance mine.

- He must be blissfully unaware of my status as a successful television anchor (I wanted him to love me for myself and not the power and prestige of my chosen profession).
- Above all else, he must be a whiz at tennis (an expert who can teach me all the tricks of a game I love so well).

In fact, the only thing I failed to ask for was that he be a millionaire. Actually I did write it on my list but quickly crossed it out, thinking I was getting a bit greedy. So in place of that, I wrote one last item:

- He must have the potential to become a millionaire.

There you have it—my list of items, which add up to Mr. Perfect. The only thing left was to pray on my wish list before bedtime for God to deliver such a man, and to tuck the list safely under my pillow.

I didn't have to wait long for an answer to my prayers.

The following Sunday, I was zipping to church in my 911 Porsche Targa. It's a car that never fails to attract attention, particularly the attention of the opposite sex. I had read somewhere that women with serious cars attract serious attention from men. In my experience, that was true.

I believe it was my flashy red and black car that first caught his eye as I dashed off the highway exit and pulled up alongside his rather nondescript model, a Volkswagen Cabriolet. I didn't know it then, but he had recently downsized from his less-than-modest Corvette. Ah, a man of substance!

I remember glancing over and catching his eye. "Um-m-m, black hair, blue eyes, and a little forelock that tumbles onto his attractive forehead, just like Superman."

The stoplight blinked green and it was time to move on. A chance encounter in an impossible situation. What was I supposed to do, run out of my car and bang on his windshield? Instead, I just let go of the moment and moved on.

As I pulled into the parking lot of my place of worship, I saw the most amazing thing. There he was, striding up to the portal of the church, my church. Could this be possible? I quickly looked him over from the top of his pretty head to a quick scan of his ring finger. No wedding ring! He was just too beautiful to be going to church alone. My first fleeting thought was, "He must be gay," otherwise some other little filly would have roped in this cowboy by now.

I moved quickly to the front of the church and looked for the friends with whom I usually sit. What a dummy! Of course, none of them were there because this was the 8:00 A.M. service, which I never attend. I usually come strolling in at 11:45. But this Sunday I was attending the early service because I was later going to the Cincinnati Bengals' pro-football game with my boss, and she wanted to leave early enough to beat the crowd.

As I reached the front of the church, I furtively glanced over my shoulder and spotted the object of my curiosity near the back. Quickly reversing direction and being as unobtrusive as possible, I took a seat in the same pew to the left of him. I looked over and smiled and he paid absolutely no attention to me. There was enough space between us to seat six people, but if anyone had dared enter this restricted area I would have tackled them before they'd made it down the aisle. As far as I was concerned this area was off limits to anyone but me. Definitely not a Christian attitude.

I was protecting my space because I knew how my pastor worked. At the beginning of the service, we would be asked to shake hands and greet those around us. Even more important would be what happened at the end of the service. We would be asked to stand and hold hands with those next to us as we sang a good-bye hymn filled with good wishes for our fellow man.

And shame on me for what I was thinking about my fellow man, and right there in church, too!

As the moment for the greeting came, this darling man reached to introduce himself, and as I said, "Hi, I'm Donna," I realized he didn't have a clue as to my alter identity, my TV persona. Believe me, I can tell when somebody knows. My first reaction to that realization was, "Where does he live, in a cave?" But that thought was quickly replaced by the remembrance that I had asked God for a man who wasn't influenced by my position. Quickly I took stock of how the items on my list had so far been matched: in addition to appearance, he was obviously seeing the real me instead of the TV anchor. ("Yes!" Three mental checkmarks on my written list.)

We both settled back in our seats as the pastor began his sermon on how to find joy, but I couldn't settle down. I found myself sneaking glances at the warm and friendly man sitting by my side, wondering if my joy might someday lie with him. It was as if God were using the pastor as a matchmaker, saying, "Okay, Donna, just reach out and grab your happiness." And that's exactly what I did.

When the moment came to hold hands at the end of the service, sparks flew from the touch of our hands. What was supposed to be a simple gesture of friendship had more meaning for us.

It was then he told me that he would like to take me out for breakfast so we could get to know each other better. Hastily he explained that his attendance at my church was a one-time deal, a chance meeting. My jaw dropped as he explained how he felt compelled to be there that day because he was going out of state and didn't feel it was right to miss church, but his own church did not have an 8:00 A.M. service.

Think about this. Neither of us ordinarily attended that particular service. This was truly a once-in-a-lifetime opportunity. Was it just fate? I began to realize there was more than fate at work when he explained where he was going that afternoon. "To a ski swap."

When I not-so-innocently asked, "Are you a good skier?" he replied, "No, intermediate level."

"Yes!" I said to myself, mentally checking off another item from my list.

As we walked into the restaurant together, the usual thing happened, only he didn't understand it because he knew nothing about me. All eyes in the restaurant turned toward us and began to stare, pulled like a magnet to the familiar features seen on TV every weeknight. It was then he quickly looked down at his zipper to see if it was open! He couldn't think of any other reason why the crowd would be staring so obviously. Comforted by the fact that all was well down there, he pushed on and we found a table.

As we broke bread, I pressed for details. Don't forget, I'm a reporter at heart and also a driver personality. I'm not going to waste time on a worthless cause. So I moved quickly into Phase Two of our relationship: the getting-to-know-all-about-you phase.

In no time at all, I learned he had been divorced for three and a half years after being married for twelve. He had no children, and, sadly, his parents were deceased. On the plus side, he would bring no extra baggage to our relationship. ("Yes!" again.)

He owned his own business ("Yes!") and definitely possessed the potential to become a millionaire ("Yes!" once more). He was poised, kind, considerate, and smart, and he appeared to be a man anyone could depend on. No macho man here, he was strong and athletic, but he began to mist up when he talked of how God worked in his life. ("Yes!" I thought as I looked up and began falling deeper into those blue eyes.)

He was taller than I but not too tall. I knew I'd fit just right under his arm if he ever held me. ("Yes!") Not a smoker, he said he didn't care much for alcohol either, for both would negatively affect his athletic training. ("Yes," I said, as I mentally kept ticking the desired items off my list.)

At that point, our breakfast idyll was interrupted by the intrusion of a local physician with an ego the size of California. He stood there, uninvited, pressing me to do a story about him on the nightly news. As the doctor droned on, I glanced at my companion. Dawn was breaking as understanding spread across his face. He now knew he was sitting with a person of some small celebrity. To me, this was further evidence he was attracted to the real me and not to my TV persona. ("Yes!")

It was weeks later when I finally visited his home that I knew why he hadn't recognized me. Definitely not a TV fan, he owned an old black-and-white set that had tinfoil wrapped around the antenna to try to keep the picture from rolling and "glitching." My own mother wouldn't recognize me on that antique.

That first Sunday morning at breakfast I managed to get rid of the doctor posthaste and resume my questioning. The most important item on my list was yet to come: could this man play tennis better than I could? Surprisingly, the answer came as I was asking another question: "What did you do for a living before owning your own company?"

"Well, Donna, I'm a former tennis pro."

("Yes! Yes! Yes!") Victory was mine! I thanked the Lord that day and every day since.

Our marriage is blissful and free from stress because we love, value, and respect each other. We stand united and understand that God comes first in our lives, then each other, then our families, and after that, our jobs. Life is so much easier to live when people set priorities and live by them.

God answered my prayers the day I met Steve Mitchell, and God has answered them every day since. In fact, I consider this book a gift from God. I sincerely believe that God has a higher goal for us than that we should just have a good day. God wants us to become stronger and more God-like. For me, that means tackling many obstacles and becoming a better person, a healthy person.

Life becomes easier and less problematic if we start looking differently at each hardship we face. Remember, they are just lessons—things we have to work through to learn more about ourselves and our abilities. Don't waste time moaning about them and crying. Just get out there and learn that lesson as quickly as possible and move on to a better, stronger and more fulfilling place. No matter how low we've sunk, or what our circumstances, we can always pull ourselves up to a better situation than ever before. No matter how bad things have been in the past, you have the power to alter your future and to change your life for the better by asking God to enter your life.

## USING FAITH TO FIND ANSWERS

If life's dealing you a bad hand, then change the game. Refuse to accept failure as an option. Remember the movie

*First Wives Club* starring Goldie Hawn, Diane Keaton, and Bette Midler? The woman who wrote the book tried to sell her novel for more than three years. Twenty-seven rejection slips later, her savings were depleted and she began feeling hopeless. However, she did not give up. The novice author went on to do what few have ever done. She bypassed the publishing community entirely and sold her story to Hollywood. Soon, three studios were bidding on Olivia Goldsmith's story. Once news of the movie deal became known, selling the novel was not a problem.

The big thing you have to remember in any time of trouble is to keep yourself motivated and keep the faith. Faith is a fire in your belly. No matter how bad things have been in the past, you have the power to change your life with a strong faith in yourself and in God.

When life becomes overwhelming, get off the roller coaster and set aside a half-day for contemplation. First remember the past, but look only at how far you've come and the great things you've accomplished. Then, rethink the present. Take a personal inventory and turn to trusted advisors or friends for further enlightenment. Finally, re-chart your future by setting your course for success. And remember to always allow for the unexpected. Excitement from unknown challenges adds the proper dash of spice to what could be a bland life.

Above all else, don't worry. You can handle anything you set your mind to. When you accept the fact that "failure is NOT an option," you are making a solid commitment to yourself to solve any problem life hands you.

# INDEX

*A Few Good Men* 229
ABC 18, 236
abuse 40, 89–90, 248
*Accidental Tourist, The* 199
achievement 127
affirmation 134–36
Alcott, Louisa May 9–10
*American Journal* 8
apologizing 70, 169
*As the World Turns* 128
Ash, Mary Kay 185
Atlanta GA 244
Atlantic City NJ 179
attitude 35–36, 42, 87, 208
awards 24, 46

Balance 192–94
Barcelona 244
*Beetle Juice* 199
Big Cedar Lake 37
blond hair 84–86
body language 153
Bosnia 218–21
boundaries 239
Bradley, Melissa 223–26
bravery 53
Brownie 201
Buchanon, *see* Bradley, Melissa
*Buffalo Bill* 198
Bush, George 46, 171, 241, 253, 260–62
business world 30

Captain Crunch 35
Carter, Jimmy 11–14
CBS 18, 138–40, 191, 236
character 223–40, 252
Cheney, Dick 259–60
children 151–52
Clark, Marcia 125, 133

Clark, Mary Higgins 247
CNN 225
co-dependency 120, 253, 266
commitment 234
communication 143–74
    four levels of 146
    men's 148, 164–69
competition 91–92
complainers 113–14
confidence 123, 125–42
confrontation 170
Connery, Sean 144–45
Conrad, Robert 143–45
consistency 232–35
courage 36, 52, 70, 105
Cousteau, Jaques 33–35
Covey, Stephen 20, 146
Cox, Courteney 128
criteria 213
Cruise, Tom 229
cynic 114

Daniels, Faith 190–92
*Dateline* 191
Davis, Geena 197–200, 210
Dayton OH 47, 78–81, 204, 249
    Peace Accord 218
De Palma, Brian 128
decision-making 67–69
decisiveness 30
demotivators 10, 96–123
determination 244–52
Devers, Gail 241–44
divorce 40, 41
Dr. Ruth 30
doubt 107
doughnut test 153
drugs 149–50, 226, 242
Durham-Jefferson, Jaruth 249–51

Education 130
Emerson College 8
Emmy Award 24
environment 35
ethics, code of 229–32
experience 131

Faith 265–74
*Family Ties* 198
fear 88–90, 101–105
*First Wives Club* 274
Fox, Michael J. 198
Frankfurt 245
*Friends* 128

Gibson, Charlie 46
Gibson, Nancy 133
Girl Scouts 201
Glass, Nancy 8
Glenn, John 255–57
goals 197–21
Goldman, Ronald 126
Goldsmith, Olivia 274
golf 30–31, 91–92
*Good Morning America* 46
gossip 43–45
Griffith-Joyner, Florence 252
guilt 119–21

Habits 61, 66, 87, 97
Harvard University 8
Hoffman, Dustin 1–3, 46, 198
Hutton, Lauren 246

Ice diving 37–39
identity 186–94, 234
*If I'm So Wonderful, Why Am I Still
    Single?* 267
incentive 90
integrity 232–35, 240

Jealousy 121
Joyner-Kersee, Jackie 241

Karolyi, Bela 16–17
Kersee, Bob 241
Kiss 46
knowledge 129–31
*Kramer Vs. Kramer* 1

Laziness 84
leadership, personal 4
lies 131–32
listening 146
Lois Lane 203
Lukey, Joan 25–26

Martyr 114
Marysville OH 148–51
Massachusetts Junior Miss 133
Milwaukee WI 1, 130, 162, 204
Miss America 62, 111, 178–82, 202,
    206, 223–26
Miss Massachusetts pageant 179
Miss Ohio 225
Miss Wareham 26, 179
Miss Woburn 181
Mitchell, Stephen ix, 273
Mom 23, 41–42, 201
motivation 77–93

Namath, Joe 55–58
NBC 191, 236
negativity 36, 111
New Bedford MA 5, 10, 56
New England Telephone 202
New York NY 138–41, 198, 245
New York Jets 55
Newport 236
Nike 135
None for Under 21 campaign 226
North, Ollie 46

Olympics 15, 175, 241–42, 252
Oprah 46, 95–96, 100–101, 113
Oscar 199
Osgood, Charles v

Page, Susan 267
perfectionism 114, 140
permission 70
personality profile 174
Peshtigo River 52
Pittsburgh PA 160, 204
plan, need for 19
pleasing others 72
*PM Magazine* 1, 3, 8, 36, 52, 130, 162,
    204
Powell, Colin 28–29

President, U.S. 14, 253–63
pretense 74–75
priority 183
prison 148–51
Providence RI 5, 85

Quayle, Dan 171–73, 254
questions 151–52

Rainbow Girls 201
respect yourself 61
responsibility 67, 69, 206
Retton, Mary Lou 15–17
reward 90–91, 132, 140
risk 70, 111, 132, 137, 140
roles 188–90, 194
Roosevelt, Franklin D. 105
Rudolph, Wilma 175–78, 196
Run for the Dream 243

Safer, Morely 140
Sarajevo 218–21
Savitch, Jessica 140–42
Scranton PA 141, 203
self-confidence 125
self-discipline 217–18
self-employment 51
self-esteem 19, 61, 126–27
self-image 61–67, 72–73, 76, 127
self-love 74
self-sabotage 234
self-talk 115–18
Seoul 242
Serbia 219
sexual harassment 50
shooting the rapids 52–54
Short-Time Susie 83, 92
Shriver, Sargent 11
Silence of the Lambs 121
Simpson, Nicole Brown 126
Simpson, O.J. 125
Siskel, Gene 2
60 Minutes 18, 140
Smith, Susan 78–81
sports 30–31
Springsteen, Bruce 128
Spurlock, Hilda 247–48
STARS 65
stealing 224–28

Steinem, Gloria 115
stress 89
Summerfest 162
Super Bowl 55
support group 211–13

Tannen, Deborah 164
temptation 235
tennis 107–10
Thelma and Louise 199
Thunderbirds 37
time 205
Tootsie 198
Turner, Ted 46, 235
Turning Point 18
TV Hotline 99

Understanding 146
Union SC 78–81
Up Close and Personal 34

Values 229–32
Victoria's Secret 198
Vieira, Meredith 18
vision 177–82, 185–86, 194, 200–10
visualization 136–37, 214, 217
Volkswagen Rock 53

Wareham MA 197
WCBS 137–40
weight loss 206–209, 211–12
West 57th 18
whiner 113
WHIO 47
White House 253–62
Whitestone, Heather 62, 65
Wild, Wild West 143
Williams, Vanessa 226
Winfrey, Oprah 46, 95–96, 100–101, 113
Wisconsin Dells 37, 131
women-owned businesses 52
Woods Hole MA 33
worry 105–107
WTEV 85

You Just Don't Understand 164

Zoli agency 198

# Resources

For more information about Seminars, Workshops, Newsletters, and Telephone Consultations, or to order additional copies of this book, please write to:

Donna Jordan
c/o Cranberry Cove Publishers
P.O. Box 606
Springboro, Ohio  45066